Huguenot Genealogies

A Revised Selected Preliminary List 2001

Compiled By
Arthur Louis Finnell

CLEARFIELD

First Edition, 1999

Revised Edition printed for
Clearfield Company, Inc. by
Genealogical Publishing Co., Inc.
Baltimore, Maryland
2001

Reprinted for
Clearfield Company, Inc. by
Genealogical Publishing Co., Inc.
Baltimore, Maryland
2003

International Standard Book Number: 0-8063-5119-5

Made in the United States of America

INTRODUCTION

This is a Revised Edition of the Preliminary List of Huguenot Genealogies compiled for use by family historians. The effort is to try to bring together in one place a listing of all published genealogies for documented Huguenot families in America.

What would qualify a book to be considered a *Huguenot genealogy*? Sometimes it can be like trying to determine how high is up. The rule of thumb has been that if the progenitor and the first generations can be documented as Huguenots, the title is listed. Many of the titles included have been listed because they have been judged acceptable at one point in time. No list is ever complete or final. Old titles will be removed and placed in the appendix of disqualified lines; other new articles and books will be included as new Huguenot lines are discovered. The list also includes a substantial selection of non-Huguenot history / genealogy books, many of which have been included. Articles from major genealogical journals have also been included.

Many titles have been brought to my attention; however, unless it can be established that the family was Huguenot, the books were not included.

One of the guidelines for inclusion are Huguenot family names listed in the Fourth Edition 1995 *Register of Qualified Huguenot Ancestors of the National Huguenot Society* and the Annual *Updates* edited by the National Huguenot Society Registrar General.

New titles and old titles are always being sought, and the interest and imput of readers are always welcome. Please forward any comments to the compiler.

A predictable frustation for many researchers will be the difficulty in locating titles. Some titles can be found in most major libraries and the Library for the National Huguenot Society, The Huguenot Society of America, and the Huguenot Society of South Carolina.

Arthur Louis Finnell
3917 Heritage Hills Dr. #104
Bloomington, MN 55437-2633

KEY to PUBLICATIONS

NGS QUARTERLY	National Genealogical Society Quarterly
NEH&G Register	New England Historical & Genealogical Register
NYG&B Record	New York Genealogical & Biographical Record
TAG	The American Genealogist
Transactions HSSC	Transactions Huguenot Society of South Carolina
TVG	The Virginia Genealogist
VMH&B	Virginia Magazine of History and Biography
W&MCQ	William & Mary College Quarterly

A

AGEE *A Record of the Agee Family*; by P. M. Agee; 1937; 330p

AGEE *The Agee Register: A Genealogical Record of the Descendants of Mathieu Agee, A Huguenot Refugee to Virginia*; by Louis N. Agee; 1982;

ALLAIRE *The Allaire Family of La Rochelle, France and Weschester County, New York*; by Glenna See Hill; *NYG&B Record*, Volume Nos 3 & 4; Volume Nos 1,2,3,4. 1994/95.

ALLAIRE *The Allaire - Dallaire Families*; by Violette Allaire; 1962; np; nd

ALIEE "The Family of Jean Aliee"; by William Heidgerd; *The Huguenot Historian A Journal of Huguenot History and Genealogy*; Huguenot Society of New Jersey; 1982/84

ALYEA / ALIEE "Alyea, Aliee, Alje; Allee, Alleen, Alye"; *The Genealogical Magazine of New Jersey*; Vol 20 No 2 (April 1945)

ALLEE / ALYEA *Allee / Alyea Genealogy*; by W. Arthur Allee; 2 Volumes, 1991; 513p.

AMIDON *The Amidon Family: A Record of the Descendants of Roger Amadowne of Rehoboth, Massachusetts*; by Frank Best; Chicago; 1904

AMMIDOWN *Genealogical Memorial and Family Record of the Ammidown Family, and a Partial Record of Some Other Families of Southbridge, Massachusetts*; by Holmes Ammidown; 1877

AMMONET *The Omohundo Genealogical Record The Omohundros and Allied Families in America*; By Malvern Hill Omohundro; Staunton, VA; 1950-51; 1287pages

AMMONET; "Jacob Ammonet of Virginia and a Part of His Descendants"; by Cliff Wood Bransford; *Publication of the Southern History Association*; Volume III; 1899

ANGEVINES *In America -- The Angevines*; by Erma Angevine; 1976; 71p.

ANGEVINE *Angevine Genealogy Descendants of Zachariah & Pierre Angevine 1690 to 1976 in America*; Compiled by Clayde V. Angevine; 1977; Endwell, NY; 399pages

ANKENEY *Agne, Angne, Angene, Aukeny, Aukenen, Aukney, Aukeney, Anguenet, ETC*; by Gustav Angne; 1978 (translated from German by Lawrence W. Jenkins)

ANKENY *Sketch of the Life & Some Descendants of Dewald Ankeny: b. Germany,1728; Came to America, 1746 & Settled in Lancaster Co., Moved 1762 to Maryland & Died in 1781. With Sketches of Descendants of Michael Walter & Catherine Ankeny*; by C. Shultz; 1948; 100+82p.

AYDELOTT *The History of the Aydelott Family in the United States*; by George Carl Aydelott; 1959; ___p.

AYMAR / EYMER; "Amyar of New York"; by Benjamin Aymar; *Proceedings of the Huguenot Society of America*; Vol III Part II (1896-1902)

B

BAILLIET *The Bailliet, Bailliett, Balliette, Balyeat, Balyard and Allied Families*; by Stephen Clay Bailliett; 1968

BASCOM *Bascon and Allied Families, Genealogical and Biographical*; by Mrs Joseph Dayton Bascom; nd.

BASS *Bass Families of the South*; by Albert D. Bass; 1961

BASS *Bass Family, Esau Bass (Revolutionary Soldier) His Brother Jonathan Bass and their Descendants*; by Ivan E. Bass; nd.

BAYARD *Colonel John Bayard and the Bayard Family in America*; by Jas Grant Wilson; 1885

BAYARD *Bayard Ancestry and Genealogy of the Samuel Bayard Family, Greene County, Pennsylvania* ; by Nannie L. Fordyce; 1954

BAYARD *A History and Genealogy of the Families Bayard, Houston of Georgia and the Descent of the Bolton Family*; by Joseph Gaston Baille Bullock; 1919

BEAUFORT see also de Beaufort and Buford

BEBOUT; *Bebout Family History*; by A.C. Flick; np; nd.

BEBOUT *Bebout Family in Flanders and North America*; by no author; n.d.

BEIGHLEY / BUCHLI *The Beighley's Family Tree*; by Walter J. Beighley

BELLINGER *History and Genealogy of Families of Bellinger and DeVeux ... Families*; by Joseph Gaston Baile Bulloch; 1895, Savannah, GA; 109p

BELLEVILLE *Jean Belleville, The Huguenot, His Descendants*; by Paul Belville Taylor; 1973; 610p.

BELLIVEAU *Belliveau Family (La Famille Belliveau) 1645-1983 and Some Legers, Pujolas and Anketell Connections*; by John E. Belliveau; 1984; 144p.

BELLIVEAU *Genealogical Dictionary of Belliveau - Beliveau Families in North America*; by Frere J. - Herve Beliveau; 1986; 939pp French & English Text

BENNET *William Adriaense Bennet Descendants and Related Families*; by Kenneth A. Bennett; Gateway Press, Baltimore; 1998

BENIN / BENNING *Francois Benin (Francis Benning) His Descendants and Allied Families*; by Eva Hardin Benning; 1981

BENEZET *Genealogical Record of George Small, Philip Albright, Johann Daniel Dünckel, William Geddes, Latimer, Thomas Barton, John Reid, Daniel Benezet, Jean Crommelion, Joel Richardson*; by Samuel Small, Jr; n.d.

de BENNEVILLE *The Keim and Allied Families*; by deB. Randolph Keim; 1899/1900

4

BERNIERE; *DeBerniere Family Papers*; by Mrs Edward McCrady; np; nd.

BERNARD "Couper Family of Longforgan (Near Dundee) Scotland and Norfolk, Virginia"; by William Couper; *VMH&B*; Volume 59 (1951)

BERNARD *Bernard "Grandparents"*; by Ted B. Bernard; np; nd

BERNON *Huguenot Genealogy of Bernon Family of La Rochelle*; nd.

BERTINE *The Bertine Family Pierre Bertine - 1686, Descendants and Allied Families*; by Dorothy Wilkerson Bertine; 1994; 504p.

BERTOLET *Genealogical History of the Bertolet Family; Descendants of Jean Bertolet*; by D. H. Bertolet; 1914; 260p

BERTRAND; "A Genealogy of the Glassell Family"; by Horace Edwin Hayden; *Virginia Genealogies*; Baltimore, 1973

BESLEY *Besley - Besley Notebook*; 3 Volumes 1981-1985; compiled by Georganna Klass Willits; (Manuscript)

BESSELIEU *The Genealogy of Several Allied Families: Frazer, Owen, Bessellieu, Carter, Shaw, Wright, Lndfair, Briggs, Neill, Tidwell, Johnson, and others*; by Charles Owen Johnson; New Orleans; 1961

BESSELLIEU *Genealogy of Several Allied Families: Frazwer, Owen, Bessellieu, Carter, Shaw, etal*; by Charles Owen Johnson; 1961; 543p

BETHUNE *History of the Bethune Family With a Sketch of the Fanueil Family, with whom the Bethunes have become Connected in America*; by Mrs J. A. Weisse; 1884; 54,39p.

BEVIER *Bevier Family*. by C. Bevier; nd.

BEVIER *The Bevier Family The Descendants of Louis Bevier, Patentee of New Paltz, New York. A Revision and Continuation of "The Bevier Family" by Katherine Bevier,1916*; by Kenneth E. Hasbrouck; 1970

BEVIER *The Bevier Family A History of the Descendants of Louis Bevier Who came from France to America in 1675 after a sojourn of ten years in the Palatinate and settled in New Paltz, New York*; by Katherine Bevier; 1916; 274p.

BILLIOU *Pierre Billiou, The Walloon, Staten Island Pioneer*; by Elmer Garfield Van Name; Haddonfield, NJ; 1954.

BILLIOU *More About the Pierre Billiou Family of Staten Island, NY with References to Osbourne, Pitney of New Jersey, etc.*; by E. G. Van Name; 1960

BILLIOU; *Jacob Dunham Genealogy with English and America Ancestry of Dunham Family*; by Sophie Dunham Moore; MI; 1963

BLANCHAN *Matthew Blanchan in Europe and America* From the papers of Major Louis DuBois (1891-1965) Revised and Enlarged by Ruth P. Heidgerd; 1979; 20p

BOBO / BODEAU "Huguenots in the Backcountry The Bobo Family of France, Virginia and South Carolina"; by Bryan Scott Johnson; *Transactions HSSC*; No. 100 (1995)

BODINE *Annals of the Sinnott, Rogers, Coffins, Corlis, Reeves, Bodine and Allied Families*; by Mary Elizabeth Sinnott; n.d.

BOISSEVAIN *Stamboek Der Boissevains*; by Barthold Hubert Boissevain; 1937

BOITNOTT *Boitnott and Related Families. History and Genealogy of Descendants of Justus and Susannah (Dishong) Boilnott*; by John W. Boitnott; 1971; 312p.

BOUDINOT *E. B. Boudinot The Story of Elias Boudinot IV, his Family, His Friends and His Country*; by Barbara L. Clark; 1977; 472p.

BOUDINOT *Elias Boudinot, Patriot and Statesman*; by George Adam Boyd; New York; 1952

BOULIER *The Genealogy of the Boulier-Balyea-Belyea Family 1679-1969*; by Florence G. Belyea Tisdale & Marjorie A. Belyea Rennie; 1970

BONTECOU *Bontecou Genealogy: A Record of the Descendants of Pierre Bontecou, Huguenot Refugee From France, in the Line of his Sons*; by John E. Morris; 1885; 271p.

BONTECOU *Bontecou Family*; by G. Norris, np; nd.

BONTECOU *The Ancestry of Daniel Bontecou of Springfield, Massachusetts A Record of Forty Successive Generations, Extending through Thirteen Centuries*; by John E. Morris; 1887

BOUCHER *The Bowshelder - Boucher Myth Discovered*; by John Holly Boucher, Jr; unpublished manuscript.

BOWDOIN *Some Accounts of Bowdoin Family with a Notice of Erving Family*; 3rd Edition; by T. Prime; 1900; 18p

BOWDOIN *Some Accounts of the Bowdoin Family with Notes on the Family of Pordage, Lynde, Newgate, Erving*; by T. Prime; 2nd Edition 52p 1894.

BOWDOIN *A Research of the Bowdoin Family in the United States*; by U. Bowdoin Marsh; 1982; 228p.

BOWDOIN "French Huguenots in Boston: The Faneuills, The Bowdoins, The Reveres"; *The Essex Genealogist*; Volume 13 No.3 (May 1993)

BOYER *Genealogy of the Vale, Walker, Littler and other Related Families*; by George Walker Vale; np; 1973

BOYER " Boyer, Bayer, Beyer, Beier, Baire - Pa Records" by Michael Alvin Gruber; *NGS Quarterly*; Vol X No.2 (Jul 1921)

BRASHEAR / BRASHEARS *The Brashear -- Brashears Family 1449-1929*; by Henry Sinclair Brashear; 1929; 170p.

BRASHEAR *The Brashear Story a Family History containing a Partial account of a Family that has been in America for well over three hundred years*; by Troy L. Back and Leon Brashear; 1962; ---p.377

BRASHEAR *Belt Brashear and Amelia Duvall Their Ancestors &
Descendants*; by Sydney M. Kilpatrick; (1970); p.147

BRASHEAR *A Brashear[s] Family History*; Volume I The First 200 Years
of Bashear[s] in America. Descendants of Robert & Benois Brasseur; by
Charles Brashear & Shirley Brashear McCoy; 1998; 320 pages

BRASHEAR *Brashe[a]r Family Branches Issues 1-34*; Published by Arzella
Brashear Spear
Indes to..; to Issues 1-34 plus Place name Index; Special project by The
Arlington House Chapter, DAR

BROADDUS *History of the Broaddus Family... In the United States to the
Year 1888*; by Andrew Broaddus; St Louis, MO; N.d.; 200p

BROKAW "Brokaw Family (Brogan)"; by Minot Pitman; *New York
Genealogical & Biographical Record*; Vol 86

BROKAW - BRAGAW *Our Brokaw - Bragaw Heritage*; compiled by Mrs
Elsie E. Foster; nd[1967] ; 829p.
INDEX, compiled by Gerald J. Parsons; 1968; 140p.

BRUYER *Jacque Bruyer: A French Huguenot and Descendants*; by Mary
Burt; np; nd

BUFORD *Buford Family in America*; by Marcus Bainfield Minter; San
Francisco, CA; 1903; p.403

BUFORD *History and Genealogy of the Buford Family in America with
Records of a Number of Allied Families*; by Captain Marcus Bainbridge
Buford; San Francisco, CA, 1903; Revised and Enlarge Edition by George
Washington Buford and Mildred Buford Minter; 1924

BURDINE *The Burdine Family*; by Dr Winston E. Burdine; nd.

BUTINS *The Butins in America*; by Oval Quist; Des Moines, IA; Apr 1969
(mimographed)

C

CABANISS *Henry Cabaniss and His Descendants*; by John Plath Green; nd

CABANISS *Cabaniss Through Four Generations*; by Allen Cabaniss

CALMES; "The Calmes Family"; *The Huguenot Publication No 35*; 1991-1993

CANDEE *Candee Genealogy with notices of Allied Families of Allyn, Catlin, Cooke, Mallery, Newell, Norton, Pynchon, and Wadsworth*; by Charles Candee Baldwin; Cleveland, Oh; 1882

CANTINE *A Preliminary Statement of the Cantine Genealogy or Descendants in America of Moses Cantine, Huguenot Refugee*; by Matthew Cantine Julien; 1903; 14p.

CANTINE *The Cantine Family, Descendants of Moses Cantine*; by Alice Cantine Huntington; 1957 reprinted 1982; 82p.

CARRIERE *Our Family Circle*; by Annie Elizabeth Miller; Hilton Head Island, SC; 1987

CAUDEBEC; *Caudebec in America A Record of the Descendants of Jacques Caudebec 1700 to 1920*; by William Louis Cuddeback; New York; 1919

CAUDEBEC; "Jacques Caudebec of Orange County, New York and some of His Descendants"; by Holdridge Ozro Collins; *NYG&B Record*; Volume 27, (Jul 1896).

CAVINIS *Henry Cavinis The Immigrant Infant and Some of His Descendants*; by Alloa Caviness Anderson; 1971; 526p.

CAZNEAU *Descendants of Paix Cazneau*; by Ann Smith Lainbart; *NEH&G Register*; Vol CXLII; (April 1988)

CHADEAYNE *The Chadeayne Family in America*; by Kenneth E. Hasbrouck, editor; New Paltz, NY; 1983

CHAMOIS / SHUMWAY *Genealogy of the Shumway Family in the United States of America*; by Asabel Adams Shumways; New York; 1909

CHAPPELEAR *The Chappelear Family*; by Nancy Chappelear; Wheaton, MD; 1963

CHAPPELEAR *Families of Virginia*; Volume II; by George Warren Chappelear; 1932

CHARDAVOINE; *The Dupuy Family: A Genealogical History*; by Charles Meredith Dupuy; np; 1910

CHASTAIN *The Chastain Family of Manakintown, Virginia*; by Cameron Allen; *TAG*; Volume 39; (July 1963)

CHASTAIN *Pierre Chastain and His Descendants*; Volume I First Five Generations in America' Southern Heritage Press, Pierre Chastain Family Assn; Indianapolis, IN; 1995

CHASTAIN *Pierre Chastain Revisited*; by Cameron Allen; *TAG*; Volume 64; (July 1989)

CHASTAIN *Chastain Family, Washington Co, Indiana Little Otter to Lost River* by Claude E. Cook; Indianapolis; 1976

CHASTAIN *Jason Coward Chastain and his Family 1076-1976*; by Chastain Historical Society (Manuscript)

CHASTAIN *Chastains Virginia Genealogy and Family History*; by Lowell B. Chastain; Elizabethtown, NJ; 1983 [to be used with care]

CHASTAIN *Brief History of the Huguenots and three Family Trees: Chastain - Lochridge - Stockton*; by James G. Chastain; 1933; p.372

CHASTAIN *Chastain Cousins: Origin of the Family of Chastain of Hall County, Georgia; Some of His Antecedents and Descendants*; by Rollo P. Stovall; Sarasota, Fl; 1977

CHASTAIN *Chastain Kith and Kin, 1780-1980*; by Mary Avilla Abel Farnsworth Milligan; Newton, KS; 1981

CHASTAIN *Chasteen Genealogy and Family History*; by Naomi Jackson Chasteen; Broken Arrow, OK; 1987

CHASTAIN "A Roman Catholic Perspective on the Huguenot Chastain Family of Chârost in Berri, France 1685 and Later"; by Cameron Allen; *TAG*; Volume 71 No 4 (Oct 1996)

CHAILLÉS *The Chaillés in France and America The Descendants of Bonaventure Chaillé*; by Jack H. Chaillé; 1995; 451p.

CHATEAU; *Foulke, Lupfer and Allied Families*; by ___ Chambers; np; 1952

CHAUDIN; "Francis (Francois) Chaudion (c1717/18 - 1799/1800) of Manakin Town and Buckingham Co, VA"; by Cameron Allen; *TVG*; Volume 40, Nos 2-3-4 (1996); Volume 41, Nos 1-2 (1997)

CHAUDOINS *Chaudoins of Virginia 1750 - 1900*; by Gloria J. Cowan Smith; Baltimore, MD; 1995

CHENAULT *Descendants of Estienne Chenault*; by Carlton B. Rogers, Jr; 1978; p.265

CHENAULT *Descendants of Estienne Chenault 1991 Edition*; by Belle Montgomery Chenault; 1992; Decatur, AL; np

CHENAULT *Our Heritage: A Record of Information about the Hynes, Wait, Powers, Chenault, Maxey, Brewster, Starr and Memoirs of many Persons, Confined and Supplemented by Examination of Deeds, Wills, Marriage, Death and Other Official Records of Many States and Communties*; by Lee Powers Hynes; 1957

CHIBAILHE; *The Ancestry of Anthony Trabue (Antoine Trabuc)*; by James A Trabue; 1992

CLARISSE; "Esther DuBois, second wife of Claude LeMaitre"; by H. Minot Pilman; *NYG&B Record*; Vol XCIV No 3, (Jul 1963).

CLARISSE *Genealogy, History and Biographical Records of the Families of Joseph Haneu & Sarah Decker; David MacFarlane & Janet Millar; Philip Henry Moore & Mary Ann Van Wagensen and Allied Families*; Compiled by W. Flora Shepard; Capital City, Inc, Topeka, KS; 1971

CLEWELL *History of the Clewell Family in the United States of America 1737-1907*; by Lewis B. Clewell and Rev Lewis P. Clewell; n.d.

COLLIN *John Collin Stem and Branches The Descendants of Captain Merwin Collin of MIlfrod, Connecticut*; by Ruth Collin Stong; 1980; Elmira, NY

COLVETT *Colvett Family Chronicles The History of the Colvett Family of Tennessee 1630-1990*; by Latayne Colvett Stanfill; 1991; 635p.

CORTELYOU *Ancestry of Two Sisters, Helen Robina Cortelyou & Carol Van Zandt Cortelyou* by J. V. Cortelyou; 1954; 135p.

CORTELYOU *The Cortelyou Genealogy*; by John VanZandt Cortelyou; Lincoln, NE; 1942

CORTELYOU *The Cartelyou Genealogy: A Record of Jaques Cortelyou and of many of his Descendants*; by John VanZandt Cortelyou; 1942; 607 pages

CONTANT *Countant Family of New Rochelle, Westchester County, New York and Ulster County, New York*; comp. by G. A. Barber; 1963

COSSART *Genealogy of the Cossart, Cossairt, Cossatt, Cozart, Cozad and Cosad Family*; by Joseph Arthur Cossairt; 1932.

COSSART *Cossart or Cozart A brief Genealogical and Historical Sketch of the Name and Family*; by Mary Ethel Tilley; 1944; 75p.

COSSART *From Jacques to Jon and Jinger*; by Virginia Shank Wilson; Dallas, Tx; 1975

COTHONNEAU / CUTTINO; "Further Notes on the History of the Cuttino Family 1687-1932"; by G.P. Cuttino; *Transactions HSSC*; No 45 (1940) and No 65 (1960).

COUILLANDEAU *DuBose Genealogy, Descandants of Isaac Dubose and wife Suzanne Couillandeau*; by Dorothy Kelly Mac Dowell; 1981

COURSEN *The Coursen (Corson) Family 1612 to 1917 with the Staten*

Island Branch ; by Percival Glenroy Ullman; 1917; 88p.

COURSEN *The Coursens of Sessex County, New Jersey* A reprint from *"The Woodruffs of New Jersey"*; by Francis E. Woodruff; 1909

COZART *Early Cozart History Cozart family from 1662 to present day*; by Paul T. Cozart; Colson Press; [1998]

CRESSON *Pierre Cresson The Huguenot of Staten Island*; by Elmer Garfield Van Name; Gloucester County Historical Society; 1968

CRISPEL *The Crispell Family of America* by Kenneth Hasbrouck; 1976

CRISPEL *The Crispell Family of Ulster County, NY*; by Thomas G. Evans; *NYG&B Record*; Volume 21; (April 1890).

CRISPELL *The Crispell Family in America*; by Kenneth E. Hasbrouck, Sr; Vol I 1976; Vol II 1984; Vol III 1989; Vol IV 1991; Vol V 1996; New Paltz Historical Society

CROCHERON "The Crocheron Family of Staten Island"; by Charlotte Megill Hix; *NYG&B Record*; Volume 111 (Jan-Oct 1980); Volume 112 (Jan 1981).

CROCKERAGUE / CROCKETT *Biographical Sketches of Colonel Joseph Crockett: A Paper Read before the Filson Club, 1908; Part Second*; by Gen. Samuel W. Price; n.d.

CUTTINO *History of the Cuttino Family*; by George Peddy Cuttino; 1982; Emory University, Atlanta, GA; 103p

D

DABNEYS *Sketch of the Dabneys of Virginia*; by William H. Dabney; 1887; 197p,index. Reprinted 1999

D'ANDELOT *D'Andelot and Belin Families*; by M. D. Laird; 1935; 60p.

DASHIEL *Throckmorton, Barbour, Jones Genealogy of these three Families .. Dashiel Families*; by Otey Sherman Jones; 1939, St Louis, MO; 87p.

DASHIELL *Dashiell Family Records;* two Volumes; Compiled by Benjamin J. Dashiell; Baltimore, MD, 1928/29

DAVANT *A place in History - The Davant Family*; by Hardin Davant Hanahan; Columbia, SC; 1972

DAVANT "Davant Family History"; by Hardin Davant Hanahan; *Transactions HSSC*; No 72 (1969) and No 75 (1970)

DAVID; *Montross: A Family History*; by John Wilson Taylor; np; nd.

DAVID *The David Journal*; Volume I (Jan - Jul 1983) Published by the Pierre David Family Association.

DEARMOND *DeArmond Familes of America and Some Related Families*; by Roscoe Carlisle D'Armand; originally published Knoxville, Tn, 1952; reprinted second edition 1986; 732p.

de BEAUFORT *Family of deBeaufort in France, Holland, Germany and England*; by William Morris Beaufort

DE BARRETT *Gerret Von Sweringen in the U S A*; by Lola Thoroughman Van Sweringen; Winter Park, FL; nd.

DE BARRETT *Family Register of Gerret van Sweringen and Descendants*; by H. H. Sweringen; second Edition; 1894

DEBAUN *The De Baun Family in America*; by Mary B. Gates; *NYG&B Record*; Volume 70; 1935.

DEBAUN *Genealogy of the DeBaun Family Twelve Generations of Descendants of Joost De Baun who settled in New Utrecht, N. Y. 1683*; by William H. Wallace, Oceanside, NY; 1992

DE BLOIS *Old Boston Families Number One The De Blois Family*; by Arthur Wentworth Hamilton Eaton; 1913, 15p.

DEBLOIS *Two Huguenot Families Deblois - Lucas*; by Frank B. Fox; 1949; 120p.

DECAMP *DeCamp Genealogy, Laurent De Camp of New Utrecht, NY, 1664 & His Descendants*; by G.A. Morrison; 1900; 77p

DECOU *Genealogy of De Cou Family showing descendant in America from Leuren des Cou of Sandtoft Colony, A Huguenot Settlement in England*; by Sarah Ella & John Allen De Cou; 1910; 217pp.

DECOU *Descendants and Ancestors of George and Margaret (Haskel Daniels) DeCou*; by Frances B. De Cou; 1970; [100 p].

DECOU *Pioneer Sketches of Long Point Settlement*; by E. A. Owen; Toronto; 1898

DeFRANCE *De France Family Record*; Edited by Irving A. DeFrance; Salem, OR; May 1968; mimographed 85pages

DeFRANCE *DeFrance Family Record 1977* Descendants of John Henry DeFrance; Part One; by Irving A. DeFrance; 181pages

DEFOREST *DeForests of Avesnes (and of New Netherland) 1494 to the Present Time*; by J. W. DeForest; 1900; 288p.

DEFOREST *The deForests of Avesnes (and of New Netherlands). A Huguenot thread in American Colonial History, 1494 to 1900*; by J. W. DeForest; 1900; 307p.

DEFOREST *Anthony DeForest of Stamford, CT 1739 His Ancestry and Some of his Descendants*; by John L. DeForest; 1983; 81p.

de FOREST *A Walloon Family in America Lockwood de Forest and his Forbears 1500-1848 Together with A Voyage To Guiana being the Journal of Jesse de Forest And his Colonists 1623-1625*; by Mrs Robert W. de Forest; Boston, 2 Volumes 1914

DeFOREST *DeForest of Avesnes and Kast McGinness*; by H.C. Burleigh; np,nd.

De GRAFFENRIED *History of De Graffenried Family 1191 - 1925*; by T.P. DeGraffenried; 282p; 1925

DeHART *DeHart Noblesse Oblige*; by John Wm Epley; 15 Dec 1997; 91 pages, Plymouth, IN

DeJARNETTE *De Jarnette and Allied Families in America 1699-1954*; by Earl Clarence Frost & May Miller; San Bernardino, CA; 1954; p.249

dela COUR DES BRISAY *Huguenot Pedigrees*; Volume II; by Charles E. Lart; Baltimore, reprint

DELAMAR *Some Descendants of Francis Delamar*; by Marybelle Delamar; nd; np.

DELAMATER *Genealogy of Descendants of Claude LeMaiter (Dalamater) who came from France via Holland and settled at New Netherland 1652*; by La Fayette dela Mater; 1882; 229p.

DELAMATER *The Ancstors and Descendants of Simon Van Ness and Hester Delamater*; by David M. Riker; Manuscript 1981-1984; Mechanicsburg, PA

DELANO see also de La Noye

De La MONTAGNE *The Montanye Family*; edited by Lois Stewart; Society of Descendants of Johannes de la Montague; Aug 1991

de la MONTAGNE *Newsletter*; The Society of Descendants of Johannes de la Montagne; Vol 1 NO 1 (Winter 1983) to current

DELAND *The Deland Family in America, A Biographical Genealogy*; by Frederich Deland Leete; Deland, FL; 1943; 414 pages

DELANO *Genealogy History & Alliances of the American House of Delano, 1621-1899, With History and Heraldry of Maison De Franchimont & De Lannoy to Delano, 1096-1621*; by J. A. Deland and M. D. de Lannoy; 1899; 561p.

DELAPLAINE; *Family History - Delaplaine*; Manuscript; nd

DELASHMUTT; *The Delashmutt Story Elias Delashmutt of Frederick County, Maryland and his Descendants*; by Virgil D. Close; np; 1994

DELAUTER *Delauter Families in America: Delauder, Delawd[t]er, DeLaughter*; by Pauline Grace Delauter Fry; nd,np

DELAVAL *The Gay Delavals*; by F. Askham; 1955; 256p.

DELAVAL *Royal Ancestry of Barnbara Delaval, wife of John Watson*; chart 11x 8.5; nd

DELAVAN *Cornelius Delavan of Stamford, CT and some of his Descendants*; by Elmer Milton Bernnett; 1940 (a typed manuscript); 94 pages with 16 page index

DE LA VERGNE *Descendants of Nicolas DeLa Vergne of Dutchess County, NY Through His Son Lewis (1738-1805)* Compiled by Dorothy Gaven; Los Angeles [CA]; 1993 revieds edition 1995; 296p

DELONG *My Ancestors*; by Dr Irwin Hoch DeLong; 1930; 99p.

DELONG *Delongs of New York and Brooklyn. A Huguenot Family Portrait*; by Thomas A. DeLong; 1972; 203p.

DES BRISAY; *Huguenot Pedigrees*; by Charles E. Lart; Vol II

des MAREST *The Demarest Family, Davis des Maresı of the French Patent on the Hackensack & His Descendants*; by William H.S. & Mary A. Demarest; 1938; 576p.

DEMAREST *The Demarest Family* by Mary A. Demarest & William H. S. Demarest; New Brunswick, NJ; 1938; Supplement I, 1942; Supplement II, 1944; Supplement III, 1947

DEMAREST *Demarest Family DeMara, Demaray, Demorary, Demoray, DeMary, Demaree, Demeree, Dimorier, Demarest, Demerest, Domorest*; by Voorhes P. Demarest; 2 Volumes, 2nd Edition; 1964

DEMAREST *Supplement to the Second Edition The Demarest Family*; Demarest Family Assn; 1971

DEMARIS *The DeMaris Tree In the Untited Sates A Record of the Descendants of Peter Demaris 1749 - 1979*; Compiled by Furman A. Demaris, IV; Baltimore, MD; Voluem I, 1979; Volume II, 1982; Corrections to Volume I 1979 Published [1979] Baltimore, MD

DEMARANVILLE *DeMaranville Genealogy, Descendants of Louis DeMaranville*; by G. L. Randall; 1921; 152p.

DEMERÉ "The Huguenot Redcoat Captains Raymond and Paul Demeré"; by Partick M. Demere; *Transactions HSSC*; No.102 [1997]

DeMILLE / de MIL *DeMille Family History and Genealogy*; by Issa M. R. Stapley; np; 1953

DEMORNAY *A Huguenot Family of the XVI Century (De Marnay)*; by Lucy Crump. np nd

DEMOURVELL *George Mason Including one line of Descent and Related lines of Demourvell*; by Martha Stuart Helligo; 1983

DEMOSS *The Demoss Family in America*; by Edith Susanna (De Moss) Caughon; 1942

DEMOSS *Sequel to the DeMoss Family in America*; by Mrs G. L. Caughron; 1952

DEMOSS *DeMoss Family History Following the line of Louis Dumas and Catherine (maiden name unknown) Charles Demoss and wives, Fannie and Rebecca Throckmorton Peter Demoss and Catherine Houseman John Demoss and wives, Jewley (Julia) Fowler and Sarah Barker and their descendants*; by Jo Ann Robertson Hornby; Wichita, KS; Sept 1977 (Updated Jan 1998)

DEPLANCQUE; "Sara (DePlanck) Monfort"; by Harry Macy, Jr; *NYG&B Record*; Vol 122, No 3 (Jul 1991).

DEPRIEST *History of the William Allen DePriest Family of West Virginia and Pennsylvania*; by Pearl DePriest; 1966;

DePRIEST *Richardson-DePriest Family*; by R. Roller; 1905; 50p

DE ROSSET *Annals of the De Rosset Family*; by C. D. Meares; nd

DESCOTEAU *Descoteau - Decoteau - Decoto An Unusual Family*; by Clifton Earl Ryon; 112pp; 1985

DESHA / DUCHÉ *Desha Genealogy A Survey*; by DeWitt C. Nogues; 1983

DETURK / DETURCK *History and Genealogy of the DeTurk - Deturck Family, Descendants of Isaac DeTurk and Maria Deharcourt*; by Eugene P. DeTurk; 1934; Supplement No 1 (1937)

DE PUI *History of the De Pui Family*; by W. R. Hoff; np; 1939

DEPUY/DUPUY *The Depuy/Dupuy Family of New York*; by Winifred Layman Fernstrom; 1997; (manuscript. Francois Du Puy and Nicolas Dupuy; 57 & 53p.)

DeREVIERE "the Family of Abrahan De Reviere of Philipsburgh, Manor"; by Donn Devine; *NYG&B Record*; Volume 112 (Jan/Apr 1981)

DEVAUX "New Information on the See and DeVaux Families"; By Glenna See Hill; *NYG&B RECORD*; (Apr 1979)

DEVEAUX *Genealogy of DeVeaux Family, Introducing the Numerous Forms of Spelling the Name by Various Branches and Generations in the Past Eleven Hundred Years*; by Thomas F. DeVoe; 1885; 302p.

DeVEAUX *History and Genealogy of Bellinger and DeVeaux & Other Families*; by L. F. B. Bulloch; 1895; 109p.

DeVEUX *History and Genealogy of Families of Bellinger and Deveux Families*; by Joseph Gaston Baillie Bulloch; 1895, Savannah; GA; 109p

DEVORE / DEVORE *The Devore / De Vore Families 1500 - 1992*; Compiled by Betty M. Mann; Lansing, MI; 1992; 792 pages

DEYO *The Deyo / Deyoe Family*; by Kenneth E. Hasbrouck, Sr & Ruth P. Heidgerd; Volume I 1980; supplement 1986; Supplement 1955; New Paltz Historical Society

DEYO *The Deyo (Deyoe) Family*; by Kenneth E. Hasbrouck & Ruth P. Heidgerd; New Paltz, NY; 1958, revised and enlarged 1980.

DEYO *The Deyo Family in France and New Paltz, Ulster Co, NY*; by R. G. Rider; TAG, Volume 49 No. 1 (Jan 1973)

DIGUES De La TOUCHE "Some Records of the Family of Digues DeLa Touche";by Annette M. La Touche *Publication of the Huguenot Society of London*; Volume XI NO 2 [1916]

DILLER *The Diller Family 1877 and Additional Data Provided by Theodore Diller, Alfred Diller, and Isaac Diller*; by J. F. Ringwalt; New Holand, PA; Nov 1877 reprinted Aug 1942

DILLER *A Historical Sketch of Michael Keinadt and Margaret Diller, his wife: The History and Genalogy of their Numerous Posterity in the American States up to the year 1893*; Staton, VA; 1893

DILLER *History of the Long Family of Pennsylvania*; by William Gabriel Long; Long Family Organization of Pennsylvania; 1930

DINGÉ *Information, Notes and Memoirs Concering Dingee Family History*; By Annie Wright Dingee; nd. np.

DISHIEL *Dishiell Family Records*; by Benjamin Jones Deshiell; 2 Volumes; 1928.

DISHMAN / DUCHEMIN *Dishman Family of Virginia*;by Mrs Foley White Harris; 1987

DISHMAN *The Dishmans in America*; by Edwin Joseph Dowling; np; nd.

DISMUKES *Leaves from the Dismukes Family Tree*; by Mattie H. LaFleur; 1960; 20p.

DISOSWAY *Ancestry and Descendants of the Nassau-Siegen Immigrants to Virginia 1714-1750*; by B. C. Holtzclaw

D'OLIVIER *Memories of the Ancient & Worthy Family of D'Olivier & Their Alliances, 1520 to 1803*; by Daniel J Oliver; [Publication of the Huguenot Society of America, Volume IV; 1915; 76p.

D'OLIVIER *Memoirs of th Ancient and Worthy Family of d'Olivier & Their Alliances 1520 - to 1803*; by Daniel J. Olivier; 76p; 1915

DOREMUS *Genealogy of The Doremus Familyin America, Descendants of Cornelis Doremus, From Breskens and Middleburg in Holland, who emigrated to America about 1685/6 and Settled at Acquackanok (Now Paterson), New Jersey*; by William Nelson; Paterson, NJ; 1897, 232 pages; reprinted c1972

DOREMUS *The Doremus Family in America 1687-1987* Revised Edition Based on *The Deremus Family History in America* by William Nelson, 1897; Revised by Edith Whitcraft Eberhart; Gateway Press Baltimore; 1990

DOVERAGE von *Our Family Heritage*; by Minnie Speer Boone; New York, 1956

DOZIER *Ancestors and Descendants of Thomas Marion Dozier, Jr Twelve Genealations of Doziers 1673 - 1986*; by Rebecca Leach Dozier; 1986

DRAGOO *History of Dragoo, Speer, Duncan,and Woodside Families*; by Alice Y. Duncan

DUBOURDIEU *Baby on Her Back. A History of the Huguenot Family DuBourdieu*; by Rev William J. DuBourdieu; Lake Forest, IL; 1967

DUBOIS *The American Descendants of Chrétien Du Bois of Wicres, France*; Parts 1 to 20; by William Heidgerd; with Index; 1968 - 1988

DUBOIS *The European Ancestry of Chrétien Du Bois of Wicres, France 1597-1628*; by Matthew Hilt Murphy; 1995; 130p.

du BOIS *Millar - duBois Family, Its History and Genealogy*; by Eva M. Nourse; np; 1928;p.407

DuBOIS *The Origin and Descent of am American Van Metre Family collected from Civil   Church and Military and Family Records*; compiled by Samuel Gordon Smyth; nd np.

DuBOIS *Bi-Centenary Reunion of the Descendants of Louis and Jacques DuBois Emigrants to America 1660 and 1675 at New Paltz, New York, 1875*; Compiled for the Family
Connections, Philadelphia, PA; 1876

DUBOIS *Willoiam, Van Meter DuBois and Wainscott: Pioneer Families of Western Virginia and Kentucky*; by Sue Streett; np; nd

Du BOIS *Documents and Genealogical Chart of the Family of Benjamin DuBois of Catskill, New York Being an Addition to the History of the Descendants of Louis and Jacques DuBois as given at the Bi-centenial Reunion held at New Paltz Ulster Co, NY, 1875* Compiled by Anson DuBois and James G. DuBois; New Platz; 1876; 104 pages

DuBOIS *The Van Meter, Du Bois, Shepherd and Hite Families of West Virginia*; n.p.;nd

DuBOISE *Genealogy, History and Biographical Records of the Families of Joseph Haneu & Sarah Decker; David MacFarlane & Janet Millar; Philip Henry Moore & Mary Ann Van Wagensen and Allied Families*; Compiled by W. Flora Shepard; Capital City, Inc, Topeka, KS; 1971

Du BOSE *Supplement I II and III to Du Bose Genealogy Descendants of Isaac Du Bose and wife Suzanne Couillandeau, French Huguenot Refugees who settled on the Santee River in South Carolina about the year 1689.* Compiled by Dorothy K. MacDowell; Aikin, SC

DUBOSE *DuBose Genealogy Descendants of Isaac Dubose and wife Auzanna Couillandeau*; by Dorothy Kelly Mac Dowell; 1972, reprinted 1981; 533p (French Huguenot refugee who settled on the Santee River in South Carolina about 1689)

DUBOSE *DuBose Genealogy Supplement I*; by Mrs Dorothy Kelly Mac Dowell; Columbia, SC; 1972/75

DU FORD see Devore / Devore

DuFUR / DEVORE *The Dufur Family from 1776 - 1977 The Descendants of David Dufur and Sarah DuFur who emigrated from New York State to Settle in the newly opened Territory of Ohio*; np, nd [1978]

DUHAMEL *Jones, Richardson, Duhamel and Allied Families of Maryland*; by Laura Jones Thompson; np; nd

DUMAS *Descendants of David Dickerson Dumas*; by John H. Wilson; Fort Worth, TX 1978

DUMAS / DEMOSS *The Demos Family in America*; by Edith Susanna Caughon; 1942

DUMAS *Descendants of David Dickerson Dumas*; Fort Wort, TX 1978

DUMAS *Sequel to the DeMoss Family in America;* np; nd.

DUMAY *The DeMay Quinlin and Jorgensen Families*; by Ida Wilson; Saint Helena, CA; Jan 1986

DUMONT *Tales of Our Forefathers and Biography Annals of Families Allied to those of McPike, Guest and Dumont*; by E. F. McPike; 1898; 181p.

DUMONT "Dumont and Allied Families"; by Eugene F. McPike; *NYG&B Record*; Volume 29, (Apr 1898).

DUMONT "Early History of the Dumont Family"; by Anne E. Smith; *Olde Ulster*; Volume 4; Edited by Jamin Meyer Brink; Kingston, 1908

DUPONT *Genealogy of the DuPont Family 1739-1942*; by Pierre S. DuPont; Wilmington, DE; 1943

DUPONT *The Early Generations of the DuPont and Allied Families*; by H. A. DuPont; New York, 1923

DUPONT *DuPont and Allied Families;: A Genealogical Study*; by Thomas H. Bateman; New York; 1965

DUPREE *The Dupree Trail: Abstracts of Documents and Miscellaneous Information Relating to the DuPre, Du Pree, Deu Pree French Huguenot Families of the United States of America*; by Emimae Pritchard Langley; Greensboro, NC; 1965

DUPRÉ *THe Dupré Trail Abstracts of Descendants and Miscellaneus Information Relating to the DuPré, DuPree, Dupree, DeuPree French Huguenot Families of the United States of America*; Compiled by Emimae Prichard Langley; Volume I, 1965; Volume II, 1966; 191 + 220 pages

DuPUY *A Genealogical History of the DuPuy Family, with additions by his son Herbert DuPuy*; by Charles Meredith DuPuy and H. Dupuy; Philadelphia, 1910; 165p

DUPUY *"The Origin of Barthélémy Dupuy of Manakintown, Virginia, and His Wife. The Construction of the Comtesse Susanne Lavillon, Her Destruction and Her Replacement, and Her Replacement by Marie Gardié / Gardier"*; by Cameron Allen; TAG Volume 74 No1 [Jan1999] pages 1-14

DUPUY *The Huguenot Bartholomew Dupuy and His Descendants*; by Rev Benjamin Hunter Dupuy; Louisville, KY; 1908; 439p.

DUPUY *Pedigree of Bartholomew Dupuy 1652-1743*; by H. D. Tector; Louisville, KY; 1908

DUPUY *The Dupuy Family, A Genealogical History*; by Charles Meredith Dupuy; 1910

DUPUY *Family of DuPuis, DuPuy, Depew*; by F. J. Conkling; *NYG&B Record*; Volume 32; (Apr/Jul 1901).

DUPUY *History of the DuPui Family, Nicholas DePui French Huguenot Refugee to America*; by Wannetta Roseberry Hoff; 1939

DUPUY "Auguste Grasset of LaRochelle London and New York City" by Neil D. Thompson; *NGS Quarterly*; Vol 66 No.1 (March 1978) (ALSO GRASSET & DUBOIS)

DURAND *The John Durand Family Huguenots; A Transcript*; by Helen F. Snow; 12 Apr 1963

DURAND *Descendants of Dr John Durand, a Huguenot born LaRochelle, France*; by S. R. Durand; 1965; 278pages

DURAND *Genealogical Register of the Family of Francis Joseph Durand*; Oberlin, Oh; 1925

DURAND *Durand Genealogy*; by Samuel R. Durand; np; nd [1971]; 278p

DURANTS "The Durants in Berkeley and Craven Counties"; by Durward Thomas DuRant; *Transactions HSSC*; Number 99 [1999]

DURIER/ DURIE *The Durie Family, Jean Durier of the Huguenot Colony in Bergen County, New Jersey*; by Howard I. Durie; Pomona, NY; 1985

DURRETT "Durrett Family"; by Mrs Bert Harter; *TVG*; Volume 15 and 16; (1971/72)

DURYEA; *Our Duryea and Tucker Lines*; by Rhea Duryea Johnson; np,nd (40pp) mimographed

DURYEA *Our Duryea & Tucker Lines*; [mimographed]; 102 pages

DURYEA "New Light on the Origin of Joost Duryea"; Contributed by Harry Macy, Jr; *NYG&B Record*; Vol 121 No.1 (Jan 1990)

DURYEA *The Charles Duryea Family A Genealogy of the Descendants of Charles Duryea, son of Joost of Buskwich, Long Island, New York*; Compiled by Harold T. Duryea; Canfield, OH 1955; Mimographed; 120p

DURYEA *The Durie Family Jean Durier of The Huguenot Colony in Bergen County, New Jersey and Some of His Duree, DuRee, Durie, DuRie and Duryea Descendants*; compiled by Howard I. Durie; Pomona, NY, 1985; 486p

DURYEE *Duryee Genealogy, 1633-1917* by ___ ; np; nd

du TRIEUX "The House of Truax, Descendants of Phillippe de Trieux 1586-1653"; by ___; *NYG&B Record*; Vol 57, 1926

DUVAL *Duvals of Kentucky from Virginia 1749-1935*; by M. G. Buchanan; 1937; 265p.

DUVAL *Mareen Duval of Middle Plantation*; by Harry Wright Newman; Washington; 1952

DUVALL *The Duvall Family in Virginia 1701 Descendants of Daniel DuVal, Huguenot and Allied Families*; by Bessie Berry Grahowski; Richmond, Va, 1931; 253p.

DUVALL *Descendants of Gideon Walker Duvall and his Brother Mareen Henry Duvall who came to South Carolina*; For the Duvall Reunion in Cheraw, SC 28 - 30 July 2000 by Charlotte Freels Duvall (Mrs John Emack); 2000; 75p.

DUVAL "The DuBall's of Maryland"; by Mary Rebecca Duval; *Huguenot Society of America Proceedings*; Volume III part 2; 1903

E

ENO *Eno Family of France and America*; (Extract from the Bassett Genealogy); 1926 36p.

ENO *The Eno Family New York Branch*; 1920; 35p

ENO *Eno and Enos Family in America, Descemdants of James Eno of Windsor, CT*; by Douglas C. Richardson; 303pp [1973]; Revised & reprinted 1985; p.320

F

FAISON; *Our Family Heritage*; by Minnie Speek Boone; New York; 1956

FANEUILL "French Huguenots in Boston: the Faneuills; the Bowdoins; the Reveres";*The Essex Genealogist*; Volume 13 NO.3 (May 1993)

FANUEIL *History of Bethune Family with a Sketch of the Faneil Family, with whom the Bethunes have Become Connected in America*; by Mrs J. A. Weisse; 54; 39pp; 1884

FAUCHÉ *The Foushee Family Record*; by Paul McClure; nd

FAUCONNIER *Allied Families of Purdy, Fouconnier, [Falconer], Archer and Perrin*; by A. F. Perrin and M. F. P. Meeker; 1911; 114p

FAUCONNIER *Pierre Fouconnier and His Descendants with some accounts of the Allied Valleaux*; by Abraham Ernest Helffenstein; Philadelphia, 1911

FAUCONNIER "The Fauconnier Family, The Falconeer House"; by John Fauconier; White Plains, NY; 1909 [*Westchester Historian Quarterly*; Volume III, IV]

FAULCONER *Thomas Falconer and His Descendants*; by James G. Foulconer; 1984 reprinted 1995 Indexed; 200p

FAULCONER *Thomas Faulconer, Descendants and Related Tidewater Virginia Families*; by James G. Faulconer & Tommy L. West; 1994, indexed, 196p

FAURE *Faure-Foard-Ford*; by Mary Ford Southworth; np;nd

FAURE *Faure - Ford - Fore - Foree of Manakintown*; by Larry Ford; nd

FAURE *The Huguenot Family of Foure and Allied Families*; by Flora Estelle Foure Richardson; 1943

FAURE *Notes on Faure Family. Fore, Foree, Ford*; by E. Byrne; 1967; 220p

FAYSSUX *Life of Dr Peter Fayssux of Charleston, South Carolina*; by Chalmers B. Davidson; 1950

de FERNEY; *William Webb Crawford Dean of Birmingham Bankers and Family Sketches Genealogies*; by Lee Forney Crawford; np; 1958.

FERREE *Madame Mary Ferree and the Huguenots of Lancaster County [PA]*; _____; np; nd

FERREE; *The Pennsylvania LeFevres*; by George Newton LeFevre; Strasburg, PA; 1952

FERRY *The Charles Ferry Family in America*; by Edward M. Ferry; Northampton, MA; 1978

FERNALD *The Universal Interantional Genealogy of the Ancient Fernald Families with Chronolgy from Creation found in he Discovered Lost Primitave Bible, Square Hebrew, Aegyptian, and other Languages* ; by Charles Augustus Fernald; Boston; 1910

FLOURNOY *Gibson Flournoy and Related Families*; by E. Madalaine Flourney; [1972];p.128

FLOURNOY *Flournoys of France from England to America 1699*; by Menifee Reed Cheek; nd

FLOURNOY *Branches from Flournoy Family Tree*; by Wayne Spiller; 1976; 285p.

FLOURNEY *Some of the Ancestors of Francis Flournoy, Sr Chesterfield County, Virginia*; Compiled by Bettye S. Rathbone; Austin, TX; 1985

FLOURNOY *Genealogies of Virginia Families from the Virginia Magazine of History and Biography*; Vol III, Baltimore, 1981

FONTAINE *From Riches to Rags to Respectability The History of a Fontaine Family and Kinfolks, Boursiquot, Maury, Glannison, Jasper, Bruton, Beall, Cox, Penwick, Vickers from 1099 to 1987*; Complied by Winston Francis Fontaine; 1987, Mobile

FONTAINE *The Journal of John Fontaine An Irish Huguenot Son in Spain and Virginia 1710-1719*; Edited with an introduction by Edward Porter Alexander; Colonial Williamsburg Foundation, Williamsburg, VA; 1972

FONTAINE *Memoirs of the Reverend Jaques Fontaine 1658 - 1728*; Edited by Dianne W. Ressinger; HSGB&I; London; 1992; 246p.

FONTAINE *A Tale of the Huguenots, or Memoirs of a French Refugee Family*; Translated by one of his descendants; New York; 1838; 266p.

FONTAINE *Journal of John Fontaine*; by E. P. Alexander; np; nd

FORTINEUX *The Fortineux-Fortiney Family (Fortney, Fortna, Fordney, Furtney) in America*; by Evajean Fortney McKnight; 1989; 600p.

FORTINEUX *An Abbreviated Genealogy Delineating The First Five Generations of the Families whos Progenitors were Jonas Fortineux - Sara Menton of Otterberg, The Palatinate*; by _____; 1986

FUQUA *Fuqua - A Fight for Freedom*; by Alya Dean Irwin; 1974

FREER *The Freer Family, The Descendants of Hugo Freer. Patentee of New Paltz*; by Ruth P. Heidgerd; New Paltz, NY; 1968; 532p

FREER *The Freer Family of New Paltz, New York*; by George Austin Morrison; *NYG&B Record*; Volumes 33 / 34; (1902/03).

FREER *The Freer Family in America*; Vol I 1990; Vol II 1993; by Kenneth E. Hasbrock, Sr. New Paltz Historical Society

FREER *The Freer Family in America*; Vol I 1990; Vol II 1993; by Kenneth E. Hasbrock, Sr. New Paltz Historical Society

FRESNEAU *Philip Freneau, Poet of the Revolution*; by Mary S. Austin; np; nd

FRESNEAU *Genealogy of the Fresneau Family*; by Rev Alfred V. Wittmeyer; nd

FREY *Levering Family History and Genealogy*; by Col John Levering; np; 1897

G

GAILLARD *Gaillard Genealogy, Descendants of Joachim Gaillard & Esther Paparel*; by Dorothy Kelly MacDowell; Aiken, SC; 1974;p.373

GAILLARD *Lessons From the Big House One Family's Passage Through The History of the South*; by Frye Gaillard; Asheboro, NC; 1994; 156p.

GAILLARD "Early Generations of the Gaillard Family"; by ___; *Transactions HSSC*; No 44 (1939)

GAILLARD *History and Pedigree of House of Gaillard or Gaylord ... and United States*; by William Gaillard; 1872, Cincinnati, OH; 75p

GALLAUDET "The Gallaudets of New Rochelle, New York"; by Rev Horace Edwin Hayden; *NYG&B Record*; Vol 19 (Jul 1888)

GANO / GAINEAU *Gano Family, U.S.A.*; by Howard Marshall Lemaster; Carlinville, IL; 1970

GANO *Gano / Ganoe / Ganow 1610-1970*; by H. M. Le Master; np; nd

GANO / GAINEAU "Identity of Susannah, wife of Stephen Gano, Jr of Staten Island"; by Consuelo Furnam; *TAG*; Vol 19 (Jul 1942)

GARRARD *Governor Garrard of Kentucky, His Descendants and Relatives*; by Anna Russell des Cognets; np; 1898, second printing.

GARRIGUES *A Genealogy of Matthew & Suzanna Garrigues [and] Their Descendants*; by Edmond Garrigues; Massillon, Oh; 1938

GARRIGUES *Our Garrigues Ancestors, French Huguenots Connected to Charlemagne & European Royalty*; by Patricia Wright Strati; 1992; 192p.

GASCHET / GUSHEE; *Genealogy of the Rev Eleazer Carver Family*; by Fred E. & Margaret Carver; Part II Allied Families Index; 1971

GASHET "Genealogy of Henri Gaschet"; by ___; *NEH&G Register* Vol (Oct 1847)

GASTINEAU *Our Gastineau Family*; Compiled by Loyd D. Gastineau; Third Edition; 1994

GASTINEAU *Gastineau Our Family* by Flossie G. Oaks; 107p 1970

GASTON *American Descendants of William Gaston and Mary Olivet Lemon*; Compiled by Max Perry, np nd

GASTON *Gaston of Chester* [South Carolina]; by Chalmers Gaston Davidson; Based chiefly on the notes and records preserved by Judge Arthur Lee Gaston; Privately printed according to the will of Judge Arthur Lee Gaston of Chester, South Carolina; np nd

GASTON *The Ancestry and Descendants of Amzi Williford Gaston II of Spartanburg County, South Carolina*; by Mary Gaston Gee; 1944

GASTON *The Gaston Family*; by Lewin Dwinnell McPherson; np.; nd.

GASTON *American Descendants of John "Jean" Gaston*; by Max Perry; Midland, TX; 1994; 405p.

GASTON *Gastons of Georgia and Allied Lines*; by Dr John Zell Gaston, Jr; Webster, TX; 1962; 94p.

GASTON *Ohio Valley Genealogies*; by Charles A. Hanna; Baltimore, MD reprint 1998

GASTON *The Gaston Howard and Wilkinson Families: A genealogical History of the Intra-married Families in the Black Belt of Alabama*; Compiled and edited by Kathleen Wilkinson Wood; Baltimore; 1976

GASTON *Our Wilson, Gaston and Huttons*; by Herman Wilson Graven; Washington, DC; 1926

GAYLORD *The English Ancestry of Deacon William Gaylord, New Light and Observations*; by Benjamin H. Gaylord; *TAG*; Volume 58, No.4 (Oct 1982)

GAYLORD "Clues from English Archives Contributory to American Genealogy"; *NYG&B Record*; Vol 16 (1910)

GAYNEAU *Some Huguenot and Related Families*; by Charles Dwight and Virginia Moore Burke Dwight; Published Privately 1975; Cincinnati

GENUNG *Genung - Ganong - Ganung Genealogy History of the Descendants of Jean Guenon of Flushing, L.I.*; by M.J.G. & L.N. Nichols; 711p; 1906

GEROULD *Genealogy of the Family of Gamaliel Gerould, son of Dr Jacques Jerauld of the of the Providence of Languedoc, France*; by Samuel L. Gerould; 1885; 1905; Supplementals 1,2,2,and 4

GEROULD *Supplements 1 and 2 The Genealogy of the Family of Gamaliel Gerauld ....*; 15 & 17 Pages; 1890

GEVAUDAN *Antoine Gevaudan of Manakin Town and His Immediate Descendants*; by Cameron Allen; *VMH&B*; Volume 73; 1965

GIBERT *Pierre Gibert, French Huguenot, His Background and Descendants*; by Albert M. Hillhouse; 398p; 1977

GIBERT; "A Short Sketch of Peter Gibert of New Bordeaux" by Anne Caroline Gibert; *Transactions HSSC*; No 66 (1961)

GILBERT *Pierre Gilbert the Devoted Huguenot: A History of the French Settlement of New Bordeaux, South Carolina*; by Anne C. Gilbert; np; c1976

GILLET *Genealogical Data Concerning the Familes of Gillet - Gillett - Gillette Chiefly pertaining to the Descendants of Jonathan Gillet, who came from Cafcombve, Somersetshire, England to Dorchester, Massachusetts in 1630 and removed to Windsor, Connecticutt in 1636. Also descendants of His Brothers, Nathan and Jeremiah with mention of a number of intermarried Families*; Compiled and edited by Esther Gillett Latham; Appleton, WI; 1953

GILLET *Our Pilgrim Progress The Gillets of Conn, Ohio, Missouri, Iowa and Wisconsin*; by Julius Ross; np; nd

GILLETT / GYLLETT *Jonathan Gillett of Dorchester, Mass and Windsor, CT and Mary Dolbere or Dolbair, His Wife*; by John Insley Coddington; *TAG*; Volume 5 (1939)

GILLETT *The Brothers Jonathan and Nathan Gillett and some of their Descendants*; by Alice Lucinda Priest; *NEHG Register*; Vol 100 (Oct 1946)

GILLETT *Gillett Families*; by Bertha Bortle Beal Aldridge; Victor, NY; 1955

GINDRAT *The Gindrat Family A supplement to Some Huguenot Families of South Carolina and Georgia;* by Harry Alexander Davis; Washington DC; 1933; 40p

GIRARDEAU "French Huguenot Descendants Share *Children of Pride* Heritage"; *Transactions HSSC*; No.91 [1986]

GIRARDEAU "The Girardeau Family of the United States; by Ronald Girardeau Crowe and Elizabeth Lee Girardeau; *Transactions HSSC*; No.94 [1989]; No.95 [1990] and No.96 [1991]

GIRAUD *The Giraud - Gerow Family in America*; by Ruby Coleman; New Paltz, NY; 1981

GOURDIN *The Gourdin Family*; by Peter Gaillard Gourdin IV; Southern Historical Press, Easley, SC; c1980; 590p

GUERARD *Memoirs of the Guerard Family*; by George C. Guerard; Tampa, Fl, 1931 [Typed Masnuscript]

GUENON / GENUNG *Genung-Ganong-Ganung Genealogy; A History of the Descendants of Jean Guenon of Flushing, Long Island*; by Mary Josephine Genung Nichols; Brooklyn, NY; 1906; 711p.

GUÉRIN "Mathurin Guérin's Children"; by Anita V. Eakin (Mrs Aldean A Eakin); [?] *Transactions HSSC*

GUÉRIN "Guerin Family"; *Transactions HSSC*; No.90 (1985)

GUÉRIN "Vincent Gurin of St Thomas & St Denis (SC); *Transactions HSSC* No. 69 (1964)

GUERIN *Guerin Family and Allied Lines*; by Denice Guerin Rice; [Indialanyic, Fl]; c1989

GUERIN *The Guerin (Guerrant) Family History*; by Opal McAdams Samuel; nd.

GUION *The Guion Family*; by Natalie M. Seth; White Plains, NY; 1956

GUION *Descendants of Louis Guion, Huguenot of LaRochelle, France to New Rochelle, Westchester County, Providence of New York*; by J. Marshall Guion IV; Oleon, NY; [1976]

GUILLET *The Guillet - Thoreau Genealogy*; by Edwin C. Guillett; nd

GUITEAU *Genealogy of Guiteau Family*; _____; np, nd.

GUYTON *Guytons Galore: From French Huguenot to Oregon Pioneers*; by Helen Guyton Rees; Portland, OR; 1986; 278p

GUYTON *Some Descendants of Joseph and Hannah Whitaker Guyton A Genealogical Listing*; 2nd edition by Guyton Bobo McCall

GRASSET "Auguste Grasset of La Rochelle, London and New York"; by Neil D. Thompson; *NGS Quarterly*; Volume 66 No.1 (March 1978)

H

HARDIN *Hardin & Harding of Virginia and Kentucky*; by Dorothy Wulfeck; np; nd.

HARCOURT *Genealogie der Familien Haraucourt - Herancourt - Héraucourt*; by Dr phil Will Héraucourt; Marburg, 1964 [In German] 51 pages

HARDIN *Ancestry and Posterity of Dr John Taliaferro and Mary Hardin Taliferro with notes on Berryman, Newton, Beheathland, Frankin, Lingo, and other Southern Families*; comp Willie Catherine Ivey; Tenmile, GA; 1926

HASBROUCK *Hasbrouck Family in America, with European Background*; by Kenneth E. Hasbrouck; 2 Volumes; np; 1961

HASBROUCK "Lineage of the Hasbrouck Family (Huguenot Abraham)"; by A. L. Snyder; extract from *Olde Ulster*; np; nd.

HAUSER *Alsatian - American Family Hauser*; by Kenneth John Hauser, Jr; np; nd.

HENNOT / ENO *The Eno and Enos Family in America*; by Douglas C. Richardson; np; 1984

HENNOT / ENO *One Bassett Family in America*; by Buell Burdett Bassette; np; 1926

HORRY *The Ancestry of Adam Jeffery Horry*; By William Horry; 1961 (unpublished manuscript)

HOTTEL *History of the Descendants of John Hottel (Immigrant from Switzerland to America) and an Authentic Genealogical Family Register of ten Generations to America, 1732, to The Present Time, 1929, with Numerous Brief Biographical Sketches, Collected and Compiled from Many Indisputable Sources: Court and Church Records, old and late Family Records and tombstones of the Many States of the Union*; by Rev W.D. Huddle & Lulu May Huddle; Strasburg, VA; 1930

HOUDLETTE *Charles Estienne Houdelette, Huguenot: The Houdlette Family 1707-1909*; by Edith Laura Houdlette; Boston; 1909

HUBERT *Genealogy of the Family of Benjamin B. Hubert, A Huguenot*; by Sarah Donelson Hubert; Atlanta, GA; 1897

HUBERT *The Migration Pattern of the Descendants of Thomas Bonner*; by James C. Bonner; Georgia; 1968

HUGER *The Ancestors of Adam Jeffery Horry*; by William Horry; 1961 (an unpublished manuscript)

HUGUS *The Immigration of the Hugus Families (Hugues) into the Muncipality of Hofgeismar (Hessen) 1686-1700*; np; nd.

de HULINGUES / HULING   *The Colonial Hulings Descendants of Marcus Laurence Holsteiner*; by Peter Stebbins Graig; Washington, DC; 1990

HUMBERT   *The Humbert Family History*; by Frances Mackin Monlux; Ames, IA; 1983

HUMBERT   *The Humbert Family 892 - 2000 (One Branch)*; by Leslie James Pyatt; 54p 2001

J

JACQUELIN   *Some Prominent Virginia Families; Edwards Jacquelin, Martha Curry, their Descendants and Colleteral Families*; by Louise Pequet DuBullet; 4 volumes; Lynchburg, VA; 1907; reprinted 1976

JACQUOT   *My Famly Tree (the Lewis Jacquot Family)*; by Howard S. Kent; 374pp; [1991]

JANVIER / JANUARY   *The Kinkeads of Delaware as Pioneers in Minnesota 1856-1868*; by Clara Janvier Kinkead; Wilmington, DE; 1949

JANVIER / JANUARY   *Thomas Januier of New Castle, Delaware 1669-1728*; by Donald J. Sublette & Elizabeth Bond Smith; unpublished manuscript; nd.

JAQUES / JACK   *The Jack Family*; a unpublished manuscript; nd.

JAQUES / JACK   *History of the Rogers Family 1643-1950*; by Mary Frances Williams; DAR; 1958/59

JAQUET   *The Pierre Jaquet Families 1490-1996*; by Martha Jaquette; np; nd

JAQUETT   *Genealogy of the Jaquett Family*; by Edwin J. Sellers; np; 190pp; 1896

JAQUETT *Genealogy of the Jaquett Family*; by Edwin J. Sellers; np; 226pp; 1907

JAQUITH *The Jaquith Family in America*; by George Oaks Jaquith and Georgetta Jarquith Walker; 1982; Indexed; 817p

JAUDON *Our Family Circle*; by Annie Elizabeth Miller; Linden, TN; 1975

JAUDON "Jaudon of Carolina"; by Robert E. H. Peeples & Sarah Nichols Pinckney; *Transactions HSSC*; No.87 (1982) through No.97 [1992]

JAUDON *Jaudon Family, An Account of (Descendants of Francois of Soubis, France & His Great Grandson Peter, Emigrant to Bucks County, Pennsylvania)*; by Edwin J. Sellers; np; 1890

JAUDON *Jaudon Family of Pennsylvania*; by Edwin J. Sellers; np; 1924

JOUETT *Some History and Genealogy of the Jouett Family*; by Joanne Cullom Moore; May 1988; 33p

JARNAT / de JARNETTE *DeJarnette and Allied Families in America (1699-1954)*; by Earl C. and Maty (Miller) Frost; San Bernardino, CA; 1954

JEAN *The Gustine Compendium*; by Gustine Courson Weaver; Cincinnati, OH; nd.

JERAULD "Gerauld (Jerauld) Family Notes"; by Kendall P. Hayward; *TAG*; Vol 28 (Jan 1952)

JERAULD *The Life and Times of Samuel Gorton*; by Adelos Gorton; Philadelphia; 1907

JERAULD *Samuel Gorton of Rhode Island and His Descendants*; by Thomas Arthur Gorton; Combined Edition; Baltimore, MD; 1985

JOLINE *André Joline and His Descendants*; by _____Joline; np; nd

JOSSERAND *L'Histoire de la Familie Josserand en U.S.A. (History of the Josserand Family in the U.S.A.)* by G. C. Josserand; (Text in English); np; 1972

JOURNEY *Genealogy of the Journey Family*; unpublished manuscript; [1970]

K

KIP *Contributions to the History of the Kip Family of New York and New Jersey*; by Edwin R. Purple; New York; 1877

KIP *History of the Kip Family in America*; by Frederick Ellsworth Kip & Margarita Lansing Hawley; np; [1928]

L

LA BOYTEAUX "The Peter Laboyteaux Family of Mt Healthy, Ohio"; by Marie Dickore; *Ohio Historical and Philophical Society Quarterly Bulletin*; Vol 12 (Jul 1954)

de LA CHAUMETTE / SHUMATE *The Shumate Family, A Genealogy*; by Theodor von Stauffenberg; Washington, DC; May 1964

de LA CHAUMETTE / SHUMATE *Our Shoemake Roots; Some Descendants of Jean De La Chaumette, The Huguenot of Rochechouart*; by Waters Strong Strong; Los Altos Hills, CA; 1984

LACY / DELANCY *The Collins and Travis Families and their Allies*; by Mary Collins Landin; np; nd

LACY / DELANCY *Family Reunion*; by Dorothy Lacey Landoll; Cullman, AL; 1987

LADOU *Ancestors and Descendants of Sarah Eleanor LaDue*; compiled by Mrs Grant Rideout; Chicago; 1930

LA DOUE *Pierre La Doue 1662-1713 Huguenot New Rochelle, New York*; by Pomeroy La Due; Detroit, Nov 1932

LAFFITTE *the Broyles, Laffittee and Boyd Relations and the Ancestors of Montague Laffittwss Boyd, Jr*; by Mrs Einer Storm Trosdal; Savannah, GA; nd.

de LA GRANGE *The La Grange Family*; by Vreeland H. Y. Leonard; np; nd.

LAGROVES *A History and Genealogy of the Groves Family in America, Descendants of Nicholas La Groves of Beverly, Massachusetts, Compiled from the Town Records, Church Records and other Authentic Records*; by William Taylor Groves; Ann Arbor, MI; 1915

de LA MARE / DELAMAR *History of the Lamar or Lemar Family in America*; by Harold Dihel Lemar; Omaha, NE; 1941

de LA MARE / DELAMAR *Delamar Some Descendanmts of Francis Delamare*; by Marybelle Delamar; np; nd.

LAMAR *Burch, Harrell and Allied Families*, Volume II; Compiled by Marilu Burch Smallwood; np; 1968

LAMAR *History of the Lamar or Lemar Family in America*; by Harold Dihel LeMar; Omaha, NE; 1941; 337 + 86 pages

LAMAR / LAMORE *Thomas Lamar The Immigrant 300 Years of Decendants* by Dennis Mott Borchers; Omaha, NE; 1977

LAMAR *Genealogy and History of Lamar and Related Familes*; by Edward Meyer; 74pp; 1935

LAMBERT *Six Centuries of the Moores of Fawleys, Berkshire, England and their Descendants*; by David Moore Hall; Richmond, VA; 1904

de LA MONTAGNE *Montaye Genealogy*; by John H. Michael; np.nd.

de LA MONTAGNE *The Montanye Family of the Mohawk Valley*; by Lois Dodge Stewart; Springfield, MO; 1981.

L'AMOUREUX "André Lamoureux The Huguenot Emigrant and Family"; by A. J. Lamoureux; *The Lamourex Record*; No. 1 (Oct 1919)

LANDON "Landon: A Huguenot Tale"; by Maynard H. Mires; *The Colonial Genealogist*; Vol 7 No 4 (1975)

LANG *Genealogy of Thomas Family*; by George Leicester Thomas; np; 1954.

LANG *Kinfolk in Germany - Kinfolk in Maryland*; by Arta F. Johnson; np; nd

LANGELL *The Langel Genealogy*; by Shirley F. Kinney; Rome, GA; nd.

LANGILLE "The North Shore Langilles of Nova Scotia"; by G. Byers; *The Nova Scotia Historical Quarterly*; Volume 7 No.3 [Sept 1977]

LANGILLE *A History and Genealogy of the South Shore Langilles of Nova Scotia*; by C. Stewart; 1977 Bridgewater, N.S.

LANIER "The Lanier Family"; *Genealogies of Virginia Families from Tayler's Quarterly Historical and Genealogical Magazine*; Vol II Baltimore, 1981

LANIER "New Light on the Ancestry of Sidney Lanier"; by Lena E. Jackson & Aubrey Strake; *Genealogies of Virginia Families from the Virginia Magazine of History and Biography*; Vol IV, Baltimore; 1981

LANIER *Elizabeth Jane Lanier (Mrs William Johnson) Her Ancestors from circa 1540, and descendants to 1982. Including the Families of Harold Drody, Alexander McIver, John Lanier McIver, William Johnson, Matthew Benjamin Floyd & Sidney Lanier, beloved Southern Poet*; by Margaret Drody Thompson; nd

LANIER *Lanier A Genealogy of the Family who came to Virginia and the French Ancestors in London*; by Louise Ingersoll; fourth printing, June 1981

LANIER *The Lanier Family of France, England, Virginia and Duplin County, North Carolina*; by Mamie Chambers Sawyer; np; nd.

LANPHERE *The Lanphere and Related Families Genealogy*; by Edward Everett Lampherel 1970 Revised Edition

LANPHERE *Jonathan Wheeler, his descendant through the Lamphere and related Families*; 1967; minographed/ xeroxed

de LA NOYE / DELANO *The Genealogy History and Alliances of the American House of Delano 1621 to 1899*; by Major Joel Andrew Delano; New York; 1899

LARDENT "The Huguenot Family of Lardennt: The Saga of a Quest"; by Charles L. Lardent; *Transactions HSSC*; NO.102 [1997]

L'ORANGE "Francis (Francois) Chaudoin (c.1717/18 - 1799/1800) of Manakin Town and Buckingham Co, VA."; by Cameron Allen; *TVG*; Vol 40 Nos 2 & 3 (1996)

LA PIERRE "The Sweet Irony of John La Pierre, Huguenot"; by W. Keats Sparrow; *The Cross of Languedoc*; Aug 1982

LA PIERRE "The Reverand John LaPierre" by Lillian Fordham Wood; *The Historical Magazine of the Protestant Episcopal Church*; Vol XL, NO 4.

LA PIERRE *Compilation if Descendants of Colonial Ancestors, The Reverand La Pierre, Benjamin Fordham*; New Bern, NC; 1944

LA PIERRE "Rev John LaPierre, French Huguenot Minister , A Horry County Progenitor"; by C. B. Berry; *The Independent Republic Quarterly*; Vol 16, No.2 (Spring 1982)

LAREW *Garet Larew, Civil War Soldier with an Account of His Ancestors and of His Descendants*; by Karl G. Ladew; Baltimore, MD; 1975

LARUE *Six Generations of La Rues and allied Families: containing sketches of Isaac LaRue, Senior, who died in Frederick County, VA, in 1795, and some accounts of his American Ancestors and three generations of his descendants and families*; by Otis May Mather; n.p. 1921

LAVIGNE / LEVINES *Leviness Family Genealogy*; by Osmund Claudis S. LeVinnes; 1969

LARZELERE / RESILIÉRE *The Swain - Tysen Family on Staten Island, New York*; by Joseph F. Mullane, Lloyd Swaim, Marjorie Decker Johnson; np, nd.

LARZELERE *Supplement 1987 The Larzelere Family of Flatbush and Staten Island, NY*; by J. F. Mullane; [1987]

LARZELERE *Larzelere Family*; by Alexander Dublin [use with care]

LATANÉ *Parson Latané 1672-1732*; by Lucy Temple Latané; Charlottesville, VA; 1936

LATANÉ *Lewis Latiné / Parson Latané*; by L. T. Latane; np; nd

LATANÉ *History and Genealogy of Peter Montague*; by George William Montague; Amherst, MA; 1899

LATOUR *Lasttures in America 1749-1979*; by Paul L. Overbay; np; [1978]

LA TOURETTE *Latourette Annuals in America*; by Lyman E. Latourette; np; nd.

LA TOURETTE "The La Tourette Family"; by Lawrence LaTourette Driggs, etal; *The Huguenot*; The Huguenot Memorial Association; Volume 3, No.3; Volume 4, Nos 1,2,3,; Volume 5; No.1 and Volume 7 No. 7; 1935-37

de LA VERGNE *Descendants of Nicholas de la Vergne who emigrated to America from France about 1721*; no author; Manuscript; np; nd.

de LA VERGNE *The Dillivans, Iowa Descendants of Nicholas Dela Vergne*; by Dorothy Garven; Los Angeles; 1979

de LA VERGNE *Descendants of Nicolas De la Vergne of Dutchess Co, NY; through Six of His Children*; by Dorothy Garven; np; nd

LE BARON *Descendants of Francis Le Baron of Plymouth, Massachusetts*; by Mary LeBaron Stockwell; Boston; 1904.

LE CLERC *Sir William Phips, Governor-General of New England and some Collateral Lines*; by Frederick Lewis Weis; np; nd

LE COMPTE "Lecompte Family"; by Francis B. Culver; *Maryland Historical Magazine*; Vol XII (1917)

LE COMTO / de GRAEF *LeComte / DeGraaf*; by Carol Harris Wbere; manuscript; Wayne, NJ; 1992.

LE CONTE *Leconte History & Genealogy, With Particular Reference to Guillaume Le Conte of New Rochelle & New York & His Descendants*; by Richard LeConte Anderson; 2 Volumes; np; 1981

LE CONTE *Notes on the Le Conte Family of New Rochelle*; by Lorenzo H. Knapp; np; 1943

LE CONTE *"Notes on the Leconte Families of New Rochelle, NY"*; by Lorenzo H. Knapp; *West Chester Historian*; 1943

LE CONTE *Genealogy, History and Biographical Records of the Families of Joseph Haneu & Sarah Decker; David MacFarlane & Janet Millar; Philip Henry Moore & Mary Ann Van Wagensen and Allied Families*; Compiled by W. Flora Shepard; Capital City, Inc, Topeka, KS; 1971

LE FEVRE *The New Paltz Le Fevres Simon LeFevre and Elizabeth Deyo married 1660 and their descendants*; compiled by Donald L. Wright; Published under the auspices of the LeFevre Family Association, nd

LE FEVRE *The Pennsylvania Lefevres*; compiled by George Newton & Franklin D. LeFevre; Strasburg, PA; 1952; 3rd edition, 1979

LE FEVRE "Isaac LeFebure (Lefevre) of Manakin Town and His Immediate Descendants"; by Cameron Allen; *VMH&B*; Vol 26 (1966)

LE FEVRE *Genealogical Chart of Isaac LeFevre, A Huguenot who Settled in Virginia*; by George N. LeFevre; Strasburg, VA; 1933

LEGARE *Biographical Sketches of the Huguenot Solomon Legare and of his Family Extending down to the Fourth Generation*; by Eliza C. K. Fludd; np. 1886

LEGARÉ "Notes on ther Legré Family"; by Lina Dayhoff Smith; *Transactions HSSC*; No.98 [1993]

LEGRÉ "Lt James Legré Family"; by Charlotte R. Carréré; *Transactions HSSC*; No.99 [1994]

LEGER "Leger, Lenud, Theus, Campbell"; by Rev F. Campbell Symonds; *W&MCQ*; Vol XIV No 4 (Oct 1934)

LEGER *The Descendants of Four Members of the First Colony of Virginia*; by Rev F. Campbell Symonds; np; 1964

le GRAND *Descendants of Pierre leGrand, French Huguenot*; ___; nd;np

LE GRAND *Pierre Le Grand in Virginia 1700*; by Louis Everett LeGrand; Baltimore, MD; 1995

LE GRAND *La Grand Family*; by Mrs Edythe Whitley; np; 1946.

LE GROVE / la GROVE *A History and Genealogy of the Groves Family in America. Descendants of Nicholas La Grove of Beverly, Massachusetts*; by William T. Groves; Ann Arbor; 1915

LE JAU *The Caroline Chronicle of Dr Francis LeJau 1706-1717*; by Frank J. Klingberg; Berkeley; 1956

LE JAU "Some Descendants of the Reverand Francis LeJau"; *Transactions HSSC*; Vol 34, (1929)

LE MAITRE / LE MASTER *Le Masters, USA 1639-1965*; by Howard Marshall LeMaster & Margaret Herberger; np; nd

LE MAITRE / DELAMETER "Esther DuBois, Second wife of Claude Le Maitre"; by H. Minot Pitman; *NYG&B Record*; Vol XCIV, No 3 (Jul 1963)

LE MAISTRE *Descendants of Claude Le Maitre*; by LaFayette DeLaMater; 1882

LE MERCIER *Sir William Phips Governor-General of New England and some Collateral Lines*; by Frederick Lewis Weis; np; 1963

LE MOINE "A Mawney Line of Descent"; by Stanley W. Arnold, Jr; *Rhode Island Genealogical Register*; Vol 11 (1988)

LE ROY *Leroy Family and Collateral Lines*; by Alexander Dubin; np; 1941

LE ROY "Le Roy Ancestry"; *Transactions HSSC*; Vol 49 (1944); Vol 89 (1984)

LE ROUX *Six Generations of La Rues and Allied Families*; by Otis M. Mather; KY; 1921; reprinted 1968

LE ROUX *Jacques LeRoux The French Huguenot and some of His Descendants LeRoux, LaRoe, LoRue*; by Emojene Damarest Chapine; Minneapolis, MN; 1939

LeSUEUR "David LeSueur (1703/04-1771/72) of Manakin Town, Virginia"; by Cameron Allen; *The Virginia Genealogist*; Vol 43, No 1 January/March 1999

L'ESPENAND "Antoine L'Espenard, The French Huguenot of New Rochelle and Some of His Descendants"; by Charles W. Darling; *NYG&B Record*; Vol 24 (Jul 1893)

L'ESPENAND *Ancestors of Henry Rogers Winthrop and His Wife Alice Woodward Babcock*; by Josephine C. Frost; np; 1927

LESERURIER *History of the Gigilliat Family of Switzerland and South Carolina*; by Robert Gignilliat Kenan; Easley, SC; 1977

LeSTRANGE *LeStrange Records A Cronicle of the Early LeStrange of Norfolk [England] & The March of Wales, 1100-1310*; by Harmon Le Strange; 407p; 1916

LESUEUR "David Le Sueur (1703/04 - 1771/72) of Manakin Town Virginia"; By Cameron Allen; *TAG*; Volume 71 No, (Jan 1996)

LESUEUR "The Castain Families of Manakin Town in Virginia"; by Cameron Allen; *TAG*; Vol 40; ___

LE VAN *Genealogical Records of the LeVan Family Descendants of Daniel LeVan and Marie Beau (Huguenots) Natives of Picardy, France, who Settled in...*; by Warren Patten Coon; Newark ?; 1927

L'HOMMEDIEU *L'Hommedieu Genealogy*; by Wm A. & P. H. L'Hommedieu; 2 Volumes; np; [1951].

LILLARD *Lillard A Family of Colonial Virginia to 1928; Including Authntic Revolutionary Service References, Early Marriage Records, Wills, Deeds, Legal Documents; Original Family Letters of Early America Lillards, etc*; by Jacques Ephraim Stout Lillard; Richmond, VA; 1928

LOUIS / LEWIS *Genealogy of the Lewis Family in America*; by Wm Terrell Lewis; Louisville, Ky; 1893

LOUIS / LEWIS *General Andrew Lewis of Roanoke and Greenbrier*; by Patricia Givans Johnson; Blockburg, VA; nd.

LOUIS/LEWIS *The Family of John Lewis, Pioneer*; Compiled by Irvin Frazier; San Antonio, TX; nd [1960?]

LOUIS / LEWIS "The Pioneer John Lewis and His Illustrious Family"; *West Virginia Historial Magazine Quarterly*; Vol 4 (Apr 1904)

M

MABILLE *6000 New York Ancestors: A Compendium of Mabie Research*; by R. Robert Murrie; Simcoe, Ontario; 1986

MABILLE "Mabie Family"; *NYG&B Record*; Vol 67 (Jul 1921)

MABILLE "The Founders of the Beck and Mabie Families in America"; *NYG&B Record*; Vol 53 (Apr 1907)

MACON *Gideon Macon of Virginia and Some of His Descendants*; by Alethea Jane Macon; revised by Jarvis Wood; np; 1956; 1979

MACON "Mason Family St Peter's Parish New Kent Co, VA"; *W&MCQ*; Vol VI; (1897/98)

MAGNY / MAINJE *The Maiden Family of Virginia and Allied Families 1623-1991*; by Sarah Finch Maiden Rollins; Houston, TX; 1991

MAGNY *Magny / Manee / Maney Genealogy*; By Kenneth B. Schoonmaker; Vol I 1986; Vol II 1989; Vol III 1990; Vol IV 1992; New Paltz Historical Society

MAHIEU *Mayflower Families through Five Generations*; by Lucy Mary Kellogg; Vol I, 1975

MAHIEU "Hester Mahieu Cooke The French Flower that Bloomed at Plymouth"; *The Daughters of the American Revolution Magazine*; Vol 107, No 3 (Feb 1973

MALBON *Malbon Genealogy, Descandants of Daniel Malbon French Huguenot of Dresden, Maine*; no author; np; nd.

MALLET *John Mallet, The Huguenot and His Descendants 1694-1894*; by Anna S. Mallett; Harrisburg, PA; 342pp; 1895; reprinted 2000

MANEVAL *Historical and Genealogical Records of the Maneval, Miller and Wilson Families*; by Willis E. Maneval; Columbia, MO; 1954

MANIGAULT *The Manigault Family of South Carolina 1685-1783*; by Marurice Alfred Crouse; PHD Dissertation Northwestern University; June 1964

MANJE *The Maiden Family of Virginia and Allied Families 1623-1991*; by Sarah Finch Maiden Rollins; Houston, Tx; 1991

MANY *41 First Cousins A History of some descendants of Jean Many French Huguenot*; Compiled by Dorothy Jones Many; West Hartford, CT; Aug 1961 [Mimo]

MANVILLE *The Manville Families in America (sometimes spelled Manvel)*; by Stewart R. Manville; White Plains, NY; nd. (a manuscript)

MARCHAND *History of the Henri Marchand II Family in America with the Descendants of Timothy Mershon, Sr of Ohio*; by Loraine B. Swiger; 1981

MARCHAND *History of the Marchand Family*; by Louis Marchand; np; 1906

MARCHAND/ MARSHON *History of the Henri Marchand II Family in America with the Descendants of Timothy Mershon, Sr of Ohio*; by Loraine B. Swiger; 1981

MARLITT / MERLET *The Mellott Family of Felton Co, PA*; by Dr Malcolm L. Mollott; np; 1981

MARR "John Marr of Stafford Co" by M. W. Hiden; *Genealogies of Virginia Families*; VOl II Baltimore, 1998

MARR "John Marr of Stafford County"; by M. W. Hiden; *Genealogies of Virginia Families*; Vol II; Baltimore; 1998

MARTAIN / MARTIN *My Ancestry; A Brief Account of the Ancestry of Lister Witherspoon and His wife Martinette Viley*; by Martinette Viley Witherspoon; np, 1922

MARTIAU *Nicolas Martiau The Adventurous Huguenot The Military Engineer and The Earliest American Ancestor of George Washington*; by John Baer Stoudt; Norristown, PA; 1932

MARTLING "Johannes Martling Pioneer One of the 150 Original Grantees of Crown Land on Staten Island"; by Ida Dudley Dale; *The Huguenot* The Huguenot Memorial Association; Volume 2 No. 2; 1932

MARYE *The Maryes of Virginia 1730-1985*; by Eduith Whitcraft Eberhart and Adaline Marye Robertson; Baltimore, MD; 1895

MARYE *The Marye's of Virginia 1730-1985 1995 Supplement*; by Edith Whitecraft Ederhart; Baltimore, MD; 1995

MARYE "Records of the Marye and Staige Families of Virginia"; by William Bose Marye; *TVG*; Volume 10; 1933/34

MATHANY *Mathany Genealogy*; a manuscript; np; nd.

MATHANY *The DesLoges Family*; by Joseph Earle Steadman; np; 1981

48

MAUPIN *The Story of Gabriel and Marie Maupin Huguenot Refugees to Virginia in 1700* (based on reserach gathered by Dr Socrates Maupin (1837) and continued from 1919-1944 by Eugene Maupin); Edited by Dorothy Maupin Shaffett; Baltimore, MD; 1994

MAUPIN *Notes on the Maupin Family, including: French Maupins, Immediate Family of Gabrielle Gabriel Branch*; Typescript; by Florence Mary Maupin; nd.

MAUPIN "The Maupin Family"; *Virginia Historical Magazine*; Vol 8 (1901)

MAUPIN *The Maupin Family*; by Nell Watson Sherman; With Allied Families; 1962

MAUPIN *History of the Maupin Family Including some of the Spencer, Via, Rice, Graves, Ballard, Genty, Miller, Hawkins, Bates, Woods, Harris, Washington, Chapman, White, Jarman, Michie, Kirby, Mullins, Pressnel, Dabney, Rea, Heard, Reed and other Families closely related and some that have intermarried with the Maupin Family*; by Ruby G. Heard Maupin; Salinas, CA; 1969; 277p

MAUPIN *The Maupin Family with Allied Branches of Miller, Harris, Martin, Ballard, Michie, Dabney, White, Jarman, Mullins, MsKenzie, Adkins, Waltrip, Jones, Near, Hall, Rea Families*; by Nell (Watson) Sherman; 1962, Marton, IL; 125p

MAUPIN *History and Genealogies of the Families of Miller, Woods, Harris, Wallace, Maupin, Oldham, Kavanaugh and Brown*; by William Harris Miller; 1907; Richmond, KY

MAURY *The Maury Family Tree, Descendants of Mary Anne Fontaine (1690-1755) and Matthew Maury (1686-1762) and others*; Compiled by Sue Crabtree West, 1971; Birgingham, AL;

MAURY *Intimate Virginiana A Century of Maury Travels by Land and Sea*; By Anne Fontaine Maury; 342p; 1941

MAURY *The Maury Family Tree*; by Sue Crabtree West; np; 1971.

49

MAURY *Maury Memories, Legends, and Records. One American Family Descendants of Mary Ann Fontaine (1690-1735) and Matthew Maury (1666-1762)*; L. M. Skeels; contains a Folding Chart; np; 1981; p.299

MAUZY *Genealogical Record of Descendants of Henry Mauzy, A Huguenot Refugee, Ancestors of the Mauzys of Virginia and Other States*; by Richard Mauzy; np; 1911

MAUZY "The Mauzey-Mauzy Family"; by Armand Jean Mauzy; *VMH&B*; Vol 58 (1950)

MAUZY *The Mauzy & Kissling Families*; by Richard Mauzy; np; 1911

MELYN/ MELEYN "Cornelis Melyn, Patroon of Staten Island and some of His Descendants"; By Paul Gibson Burton; *NYG&B Record* Volume 68 No.1,2,3,4; [1937]

MELYN "The Antwerp Ancestry of Cornelis Melyn"; by Paul Gibson Burton; *NYG&B Record*; Volume 67 [Apr 1936]

MERKLEN / MERKEL *Synopsis Merkels Freüdschaft 1435-1977*; by Norton W. Merkel; Pennsylvania; [1977]

MERKLEN / MERKEL *History of the Grim Family of Pennsylvania and its Associated Families*; by William Gabrie Long; np; 1934

MERSEREAU "Mersereau Family Genealogy"; by Henry Lawrence Mersereau; *NYH&B Record*; Vol 27 [Oct 1896, Jan & Apr 1897]

MERSHON *Story of the Forefathers of Oliver Francis Mershon, M.D., as told by Himself*; edited by Grace Lucile Olmstead Mershon; Rahway, NJ; 1946; 227p

MESEROLL *One Meseroll Genealogy 319 years and twelve generations in America*; by David B. Meseroll, JR; np; 1982

MERSHON *My Folks; Story of the Forefathers of Oliver Francis Mershon, MD, as told by Himself*; by Grace L. O. Mershon; np; 1946

MERSHON *Our Pioneers East and West of the Mississippi Peter Merchon and His Descendants*; by Grace Lucile Olmstead Mershon; np; nd.

MERSHON *Our Pioneers East and West of the Mississippi Henry Mershon II and His Descandants*; by Grace Lucile Olmstead Mershon; np; nd.

MERSHON *The Mershon Genealogy Story Part I Houghton Mershon and His Descandants*; by Grace Luclie Olmstead Mershon; np; nd.

MERSHON *Our Pioneers East and West of the Mississippi Thomas Mershon and His Descandants, and Daughters of Henry II*; by Grace Lucile Olmstead Mershon; np; nd.

MESEROLE *The Meseroles of Green Point*; by Adrian Messerole [Chart in the New York Public Library]

MESEROLE *The Meserole Family of Green Point, NY*; by Clinton Brown; nd

MESUROLLE / MESUROLE *One Meseroll Genealogy"; by David B. Meseroll, Jr; np; 1982*

METTETAL *Genealogical Record of the Mettetal Family 1728-1966*; by Della Mettetal Kuster (Mrs William); Detroit, MI; 1965 (a mansucript)

MICHAUX "The Huguenot Abraham Michaux and Descendants"; by J. D. Eggleston; *Genealogies of Virginia Families from the Virginia Magazine of History and Biography*; Vol IV; Baltimore; 1981

MICHAUX *The Ancestry of William Clopton of York County, Virginia*; by Lucy Lane Erwin; np; nd.

MICHELET / MICKLEY *The Genealogy of the Mickley Family in America*; by Minnie F. Mickley; Mickley, PA; 1893

MICHLET *Sleaten Michelet Genealogish Personal Historiske Meddelser*; by S. H. Finne Gronn; Christiana; 1919 (in Norwegian)

MICOU "Paul Micou, Huguenot Physician and His Descendants"; by The Rev Paul Micou; *VMH&B*; Vol. XLVI [Oct 1938]; Vol.XLVII [Jan 1939]

MICOU "Paul Micou, Chyrurgeon"; by Elizabeth Hawes Ryland; *W&MQ*; Apr 1936

MICOU *Colonel Moore Fountleroy His Ancestors and Descendants*; by Juliet Fauntleroy; np; nd.

MILLER *The Huguenot Millers A Family History*; by Margaret Miller White; Fulton, MS; 1986

MOLLETT *The Mallett Family of Massachusetts, Maine*; by Rev Chas N. Sinnett; np; [1923]

MONTAGUE *History and Genealogy of Peter Montague of Nansemond and Lancaster Counties, Virginia and his Descendants 1621 -1894*; by George William Montague; 1894, Amherst, Mass

MONTAGUE *History of the Sage & Slocum Family of England and America, including Allied Families of Montague, Waton (& Others)*; by H. Whittemore; 1908; 95p

MONTFOORT *The Monfoort Family of New York and New Jersey*; by Fred Sisser, III; Somerville, NJ; 1969

MONTFOORT *The Wyckoff Family in America*; by Wycoff Assn in America; Summit, NJ; nd.

MONNET *Monnet Family Genealogy. An Emphasis of a Noble Huguenot Heritage Somewhat of the First Immigrants Isaac and Pierre Monnet*; by Orra Eugene Monnette; 3 Volumes; np; 1911

MONTAGUE *Meeting of the Montague Family at Hadley, Mass. 1882*; Edited by R. Montague; 1882

MONTAGUE *History & Genealogy of the Montague Family American Descendants from Richard Montague of Hadley, Mass & Peter of Lancaster Co, VA, With Genealogical Notes of Other Families by the name of Montague*; Compiled by George William & W. L. Montague; np; 1886

MONTAGUE *The Ancestors and Descandants of James Montaney (1799-1857) of Oppenheim, Fulton County, New York. A Genealogical History of the Montana Branch of the Montanye Family, Descended from Dr Johannes de la Montagne (1595-1670)*; by Lois Stewart; Baltimore, MD; 1982

MORAGNE *Moragnes in America and Related Families*; by Bessie W. Quinn and Nell H. Howard; Birminghan, AL; nd.

MORAGNES *Moragnes in America and Related Families*; by Nell H. Howard & Bessie W. Quinn; Birmingham, AL; 1973; 566p A detailed history of the Moragne Family Decendant from Pierre Moragne & Cecile Bayle, who came from France to Abbeville District, SC prior to the Revolution.

MOTT *The French Connection of Robert J. Mott, The Ancestral Lines*; by John & Rowena Allen; np; [1993]

MOUNIER "The Mounier Family"; by Frances L. Gay; *Transactions HSSC*; No.101 [1996]

N

NAUDAIN *Descendants of Elias Naudain, The Huguenot Beginning 1655*; by Warner Woodward Naudain; np; 1988

NAUDIN "The Naudin / Nodine Family"; by Adele M. Altomare; *The Genealogist*; Volume 4, No 2 Fall 1983

NAUDIN / NODINE *Naudin (Nodine), Tourneur, De Vaux and Allied Families*; by George L. Waters; Lincoln, NE; [c1935]

NOEL *Emigrant Cornelius Noel from Holland to Virginia. His Descandants in America*; Volume 5, Part four, Book 1,2,&3; by Henry Reginald and Clara (Hambleton) Noel; *Pedigrees, Histories and Family Records*; by J. N. Weeks; 3 Volumes; np; 1980

NOEL *John and Ann Noel, being Volume four, Part two, Chapter three of Descendants of Emigrant Cornelius Noel*; by J. N. Weeks; 1978; 208pp

53

NOEL *Pedigree Charts showing the Ancestry of Floyd Clark Noel Family names included Hambleton, Roberts, Coray etc*; 70pp typewritten and some hadwritten sheets; [c1945]

NOEL *Volume Four: James and Elizabeth (Evans) Noel*; Parts 1-4; by J. N. Weeks; np; 1978

O

OGIER "Ogier Genealogical Notes"; __; *Transactions HSSC*; No.77 [1972]

OGIER "Ogier Family"; by Mary Bayliss; *Transactions HSSC*; No.101 [1996]

ORANGE *Orange Family of Henrico, Cumberland & Amelia*; by Bayne Palmer O'Brien; np; 1977

ORANGE *Oranges of Virginia*; by Linwood E. Orange; np; nd

OZIAS *History of the Osio, Osius, Ozias Families*; by Albert Lawrence Rohrer; np; 1943

P

PALISSY *Palissy the Potter, Huguenot Artist & Martyr*; by C. L. Brightwell; np; nd

PANKEY *John Pankey of Manakin Town, Virginia, and His Descendants*; Volume One; by George Edward Pankey; Ruston, LA; 1969

PANKEY *John Pankey of Manakin Town, Virginia, and His Descendants*; Volume II; by George Edward Pankey; Ruston, LA; 1972

PANKEY *John Pankey of Manakin Town, Virginia, and His Descendants*; Volume III; by George Edward Pankey; Ruston, LA; 1981

PANKEY *The Pankey Family of Virginia 1635-1968*; by William Russell Pankey; Richmond, VA; [1968]

PANKEY *This is From my Heart*; by Rev Dana M. Pankey

PARDEE *Genealogy of One Line of the Pardee Family & some Memoirs*; by Aaron Pardee; np; 1896; 69pp

PARDEE *Pardee Genealogy*; by D. L. Jacobus (editor); np; 1927; 693pp

PARMENTER "Further Notes on the English Background of John Parmenter of Sudbury and Roxbury, Massachusetts"; by Ralph Rarmenter Bennett; *NEH&G Register*; Vol 147 (Oct 1993)

PARMENTER *Genealogical Records of Parmenter, Richardson (and Other) Families*; by E. E. Parmenter; 1937

PARMENTER *Pioneer Parmenters of America*; by Clifford A. Parmenter; Vol II No 3 (Jun 1963)

PARMENTER *Parmenl[i]ers of France, England and America*; 22pp, mimeo; nd

PAYZANT / PAISANT *The Payzant and Allied Jess and Juhan Families in North America*; by Marion M. Payzant; Wollaston, MA; 1970

PERDUE *Our Family Heritage The Perdues of the Eastern Shore of Maryland 1563 to Present*; by Edward M. Perdue; 680p; 1988;

PERONNEAU "Perinneau of South Carolina"; by Michael Jenkins Huton; *Transactions HSSC*; Number 89; [1984]

PERRAULT / PERROW "Preliminary Notes on the Perrault - Perrow Family of Roi Guillaume"; by Cameron Allen; *TVG*; Vol 8 no.2 (Jun 1964); No.3 (Jul 1964); No. 4 (Oct 1964)

PERRIN *Genealogy of the Perrin Family*; by Glover Perrin; 224p; 1885

PERRIN *The John Perrin Family of Rehoboth, Massachusetts*; by Stanley Ernest Perin; Baltimore; 1974

PERRIN *Daniel Perrin "The Huguenot" & His Descendants in America of the Surnames Perrine, Perine & Prine 1665-1910*; by Howland Deleno Perrine; South Orange, NJ; 547pp; 1910

PERRIN *Daniel Perrin "the Huguenot" and his Descendants in America*; by C. E. Perrine, James A. Perrine and Ollie Negley Kern; June 1942

PERRIN *Allied Families of Purdy, Fauconnier [Falconer] Archer & Perrin*; by A. F. Perrin and M. F. P. Meeker; 1911; 114p

de PEYSTER *History of the Bringhurst Family with notes on the Clarkson, DePeyster and Boude Families*; by Josiah Granville Leach; Philadelphia; MDCCCCI

PIAT *The Pyatt - Delp Family Connections* by Leslie James Pyatt; 29 Jan 1992

PIERET *History of Some of the Ancestors and Descendants of Samuel Mortimore Myers II in America 1635 - 1973*; by Samuel M. Myers; Stillwater, OK; 23 Jul 1973

PICKENS / PICKON *Pickens Families of the South*; by E. M. Sharp; Memphis, TN; 1966

PICKENS *Cousins Monroe's History of the Pickens Family*; by Monroe Pickens, revised by Kate Pickens Day; Easley, SC; 1951

PICKENS *The Fighting Elder, Andrew Pickens 1738-1817*; by A. N. WARING; 1962

PINEAU / PINEO *Andrew Newcomb 1618-1686 and His Descendants*; by Bethuel Merritt Newcomb; New Haven, CT; 1923

PINTARD *Pintard, Stelle, Chronology includes VanVorst, Marselis, Hutchins*; by Tempe Fenn Crosby; 2000; Baton Touge, LA

POINSET *John / Jean Poinset (-by1739) of Burlington, New Jersey, Pierre Poinset l'ainé (-1699) of Charles Town, South Carolina*; by Doris Jean Post Poinsett; Bowie, MD;130pp; 1998

56

POINSETT *Genealogy of a Poinsett Family from the Atlantic Seacoast to the Colorado Rockies with Notes on the Worrell and Braamharr Families*; by Charles L. Ralph; second edition; Ft Collins, Co; 1998

POINSETT *The Poinsetts of New Jersey*; by Charles L. Ralph; Ft Collins, CO; 1994

POINSETT *The Pionsett Families of Carolina and West Jersey*; by Charles L. Ralph

POINSETT *Additions and Corrections to Previously Published Information: Carolina Beginnings of the Poinsett Family*; by Elizabeth Christie Oliveros; np; np

POINSETT "Some Descendants of Pierre Poinsett Huguenot Immigrant"; by Rev Robert Lovell Oliveros; *Transactions HSSC*; No.85 [1980]

POINSETT "Poinsett Genealogy: Aditions and Corrections also Descendants of Christopher Samuel Lovell; by Ethel Wannamaker Dominick; *Transactions HSSC*; NO.86 [1981]

POISNETT *Poinsett Family of South Carolina: The First Five Generations of the Family of Pierre Poinsett l'ainé Huguenot Immigrant*; by Elizabeth LaRoche Christie Oliveros; *Transactions HSSC* Number 104 [2000]

POITEVENT "Antoine Poitevent and Some Others"; by Isabell Bardale; *Transactions HSSC*; NO 87 [1982]; pages 70-76

POITEVENT *Poitevent Genealogy*; by Isabel Thomas Poitevent Barkdale Maynard; Birmingham, Aug 1967 [Manuscript]

PORCHER "Porcher A Huguenot Family of Ancient Lineage"; by Catherine Cordes Porcher Porcher; *Transactions HSSC*; No. 81; 1976

PORCHER "Porcher A Huguenot Family of Ancient Lineage"; by Catherine Cordes Porcher; *Transactions HSSC*, No 81; [1976]

POSEY *Posey Family in America*; by Lloyd Franklin Posey & Betty Sue Drake Posey; np; 1971

POSEY *The History of the Posey Family in Europe and the United States*; no author; np; nd.

POSEY *Posey, Wade, Harrison and Other Family Connections*; by James Wade Emison; Part IV [1969]

POTELL *The Postel-Postell-Posell Family in America*; by Francis Boeing Postelle; np; nd.

POYAS "Poyas Descandants"; by Myrtle Kershan Pelayo; *Louisiana Genealogical Register*; Vol 1 No 4 (1946)

POYAS *Pioneering with the Beville and Related Families in South Carolina, Georgia and Florida*; by Asselia Stobhar Lichliter; np; 1982

PRAA / PRAT "Praa-Bennet Family Notes"; by John Reynolds Totten; *NYG&B Record*; Vol 65, (Oct 1934)

PROVOST *A Record of the Descendants of Nicolas Provst*; by Kennell P. Brown; 56p; 1957

PROVOOST *Genealogical Notes of the Provoost Family of New York*; by E. R. Purple; np; 32pp; 1875

PROVOOST *Biographical & Genealogical Notes of the Provost Family, From 1545-1895*; by A. J. Provost; 147p; 1895

PROVOOST "History of the Provoost Family of New Amsterdam and Colonial New York from 1545 to 1724"; by Andrew J. Provost; *NYH&B Record*; Vol 34 (Oct 1958)

PROVOOST "Biographical and Genealogical Sketch of David Provost of New Amstradam and some of His Descendant"; by Edwin R. Purple; *NYH&B Record*; Vol 6 (Jan 1875)

PURVIANCE *Seldens of Virginia and Allied Families*; by Mary Selden Kennedy; Vol 1; np; 1911

PYATT *The Pyatt - Delp Family Connections*; by Leslie James Pyatt; Fort Worth, Tx; 1992

Q

QUINTARD The Quintard Family in America"; by Frederich Quintard Boyer and Herbert Armstrong; *NEH&G Register*, Vol 109 (Jul 1955)

R

RANC *The Ranks of the Rancks A Ranks / Rank Family History and Genealogy*; by J. Allen Ranck; np; 1978

RANCK/ RANC *Ranck/Rank/ronk/Runk Families Genealogical Register of the first six generations of descendants of Hans Valentine and Margaretha (Philipps) Ranck. A Couple with Roots in Germany and with three Children eventually locating in Lancaster County, Pennsylvania*; Compiled by John H. Ronk; July 1998; Spring Mills, PA

RAVENEL *Ravenel Records. A History and Genealogy of the Huguenot Family of Ravenel, of South Carolina; with some incidental accounts of the parish of St Johns Berkeley, which was their principal location*; by Henry Edmund Ravenel; Atlanta, GA 1898; 279p

RAVENEL *Ravenel Records Supplements A, B, C, and D*; by William Jervey Ravenel; Charleston, SC; 1964-68

RAVENEL *Ravenel Records History and Genealogy of the Huguenot Family of Ravenel of South Carolina; with some Incidental Accounts of the Parish of St John's Berkeley, Their Principal Location*; by H. E. Ravenel; 279p; 1898

RAPALJE "Joris Janzsen Rapelje of Valenciennes and Catelyntje Jeronimus Trico of Pry"; by George E. McCracken; *TAG*; Vol 48 (Apr 1972)

REMBERT *Remberts by way of South Carolina*; by Sallie Henritta Rembers & L. A. "Brooks' McCall; np; 1979

REMBERT "Early Generations of the Rembert Family of South Carolina"; by Caroline T. Moore; *Transactions HSSC:* No 68 (1963)

REMBERT *Rembert, Brown, Rucker, Ham, Mann and KIng Families*; Published by Sarah Jean Owen Dunaway; Atlanta, GA, 1993 [Some Descendants of André Rembert and Anne Bressan]

REMY *The Remy Family in America*; by Bonnelle William Rhamy; Fort Wayne, IN; 1942

RENAUDET "A Genealogical Account of the Families of Renaudet and Hoogland as taken from Dr Renaudt book Aug 6 1788 Philadelphia"; *Genealogies of Pennsylvania Families*; Vol III; Baltimore, 1982

RENO *Reno and Apsaalooka Servied Custer*; by Ottie W. Reno; 1997

RENO *Genealogy of Smith - McAlevy & related Families*; Nora Duke Bailey, Research; Roscoe & Virginia Smith Compilers; Vol II, Baltimore, 1976

RENO "Some Forebears and Descandants of Lewis Reno, Huguenot Immigrant to Virginia"; by William L. Reno; *The Detroit Society for Genealogical Research Magazine;* Vol 36 No.1 (Fall 1972), No.2 (Winter 1972), No.3 (Spring 1973) and No.4 (Summer 1973) [Use With Care]

RENO *Some Forebears and Descendants of Lewis Reno*; by W. L. Reno, Jr; np. nd

RENO *The Reno Family*; by Sherman Reno; np; nd

RENOLL *Daniel Renoll Huguenot and Some of His Descendants*; by Katherine E.S. Morris; Petersburg; 1969

RESILIÉRE see also LARZELERE

RESSEGUIE *Resseguie Family History and Genealogical Record of Alexander Resseguie of Norwalk, CT and four Generations*; by John E. Morris; Hartford, CT; 1888

RETIEF *Die Retief - familie in Suid-Afrika*; by Deur Dr P.J. Retief; Pretoria, South Africa; June 1971

RETTEW *Genealogy of the Rettew's Family (1658-1986) The French Huguenot and His Descendants*; by Rae Edna Rettew; Gordonville, PA; 1986

REVERE "French Huguenots in Boston:the Faneuills, the Bowdoins, the Reveres"; *The Essex Genealogist*; Volume 13 No.3 (May 1993)

REQUA *The Family of Requa 1678-1898*; by A.C. Requa; 102p; 1898

RIBLET *Ancetral History and Character Sketches of the Riblets*; by Clarence E. Ribet; np; 1953

RIBLET *Descendants of Christian Riblet and his son Bartholomew*; by David Shull & Laura Shull; Philadelphia, 1925

RICAUD *The Ricaud Family 1640-1976*; by Margaret LcLaurin Ricaud Kelly; Baltimore, Md; 1976

de RICHEBOURG *The Reverend John Graham of Woodbury, Connecticut and His Descendants*; by Helen Graham Carpenter; Chicago, 1942

de RICHBOURG "The Richbourg Family of South Carolina"; by Sam J. Ervin Jr; *Transactions HSSC*; No 78, (1973)

RICHBURGS *The Huguenot Trail Descendants of The Reverend Claude Philippe de Richebourg and His Wife Anne Chastain*; By William C. Simpson, Jr.; np nd.

RIVOIRE / REVERE *A few Generations on Three American Branches of Revere Ancestry*; by H. E. Revere; np; 1956

RIVOIRE / REVERE "Some New Information about the Ancestry of Paul Revere"; by André J. Labatut; *NEH&G Register*; Vol CXLIII, Jul 1989)

RIVOIRE / REVERE "The Revere Family"; by Donald M. Nielson; *NEH&G Register*; Vol CXLV, (Oct 1991)

ROBERDEAU *Genealogy of the Roberdeau Family, Including a Biography of General Daniel Roberdeau of the Revolutionary Army and the Continental Congress and Signer of the Articles of Confederation*; by Roberdeau Buchanan; Washington,DC; 1876

ROBERT *Our Family Circle*; by Annie Elizabeth Miller; Linden, TN; 1975

ROGERS *Jean Rogers, French Huguenot and His Descandants*; by Marion Rogers; np; 1969

ROHRER *John Rohrer of Lancaster County, Pennsylvania*; by Albert L. Rohrer; Maplewood, NJ; 1941

ROOT *Root Genealogical Record 1600-1870 Comprising the History of the Root & Roots Family in America;* by James Pierce Root; 553p; 1870.

ROOTE / ROOT *Roote - Root Route of the Roots, and Collateral Families*; by Ferne K. Patterson; np; 1982

ROQUEMORE *The Roquemore Report for 1967*; by Josephine Costello Huftaker; np; [1967]

de ROSSET *Annals of the De Rosset Family, Huguenot Immigrants to the Province of North Carolina Early in the Eighteenth Century*; by Catherine DeRosset Mears; np; nd

de ROSSET *De Rossett Family Direct Line of Descent*; by Ludlow Potter Strong; np; nd.

RUCKER *The Rucker Family Genealogy, with Ancestors, Descendants & Connections*; by S. R. Wood; 558p; 1932

RUCKER *History of the Rucker Family and Their Descendants*; by Edythe Johns Rucker Whitley; Nashville, TN; 1927

RULON *Rulon (Rouillon) Family History*; by Mrs Marion Reynolds; Elwod, IN; 1969

RULON *The Rulon Family & Their Descendants*; by John C. Rulon; np; 1870

RUNYAN *Tracking Barefoot Runyan Descendants of Isaac Barefoot Runyan ... from the Shenandoah Valley through Tennessee and Alabama...*; by Marie Runyan Wright; 1980; 292pp

RUNYON   *Up the Runyon / Runion/ Runyan Tree and Supplement to Tracking Barefoot Runyan*; by Marie Runyan Wright; np; 1993

RUNYON   *Runyon Genealogy A Genealogy of the Runyon Families who settled Early in Kentucky, North Carolina, Virginia and West Virginia*; by Robert & Amos Runyon; Brownsville, TX 1955

RUNYON   "Runyon - Runyan Family (New Jersey)"; by Col Calvin I. Kephart; *NGS Quarterly*; Vol XXIX (1941)

RUTAN   *A Rutan Family Index*, by James J. Keegan; Bowie, MD, 1996

RUTAN   *A Second Rutan Family Index*; by James J. Keegan; Bowie, MD; 1997

RUTAN *The Rutan Family in America. Gathered from records in America and France as well as from information and papers obtained from members of the family*; By Herbert A. Fisher; Bloomfield [NJ]; n.d.

S

SALLÉ   *The Family History of the French Huguenot Abraham Sallé and his descendants*; by Jack Dalton Bailey; Harrodsburg, KY; 1992

SALLEÉ   *Family History of Harris, Patterson, Poer & Collateral Lines*; by Lois Harris Redding; np; 1975.

SALLÉ   *Henry Hardin Sallé*; by Floyd Beverly Bolton; np; nd

SANXAY   *The Sanxay Family and Descendants of Rev Jacques Sanxay, Huguenot Refugee to England in 1685*; by Theodore F. Sanxay; np; 1907

SASIN / SASSIN   "Francois Sasin/Sassin of Manakin Town: The First Six Generations of the Sissin/Sasseen Family in America"; by Cameron Allen; *TAG*; Vol 37, No1 through No.4 (1993)

SCHWING   *The First Five Generations of the Swing Family in America*; by Albert H. Swing; np; 1961

SEAY *Descendants of Abraham Seay and Seay Miscellany*; by Burwell Warren Seay, IV; Volume II; np; nd.

SELOVER *Selover - Slover Family Genealogy*; by Mabel J. Hadler; First edition 1941; Second edition; 1968; Typed Manuscript, microfilmed.

SELOVER "Slocer (Seloover) Family"; *The Genealogical Magazine of New Jersey*; Vol XLI (1966)

SELLAIRE see also ZELLER

SEVIER *Sevier John 1744-1815*; by Mary Boyce Temple; np; nd

SEVIER see also XAVIER

SEVIER *Notable Southern Families, Volume 10*; by Zella Armstrong; 1926, repinted 1993

SHUEY *History of the Shuey Family in America, From 1732 to 1876*; by D. B. Shuey; 279p; 1876

SHUEY *History of the Shuey Family in America 1732-1919*; by D. B. Shuey; 2nd Edition; 381p; 1919

SHUMATE *Ancestors and Descendants of William Riley Shumate, 1777-1979*; by Norma P. Evans; np; 1979

SHUMATE *The Shumate Family: A Genealogy*; by Theodor Freidrich von Stauffenberg; Washington, DC; 1964

SHUMATE *History of the Shumate Family Kentucky Pioneers*; by Robert S. Riley; 1992; KY

SHUMAY   see also CHAMOIS and de La Chaumette

SHUMWAY *Genealogy of the Shumway Family in the U.S.A.*; by Asabel Adams Shumway; New York; 1909

SICARD "Early History of the Sicard - Secor Family"; by Henry David Gray; *NYG&B Record*; Vol LXVIII No.4 (Oct 1937)

SIGOURNEY *Genealogy of the Sigourney Family*; by H. H. W. Sigourney; np; 31pp; 1857

SIMON *Thomas Grange Simons III, His Forebears and Relations*; by Robert Bentham Simons; Charleston, 1954

SOBLETS "The Soblets of the European Refuge Ancestral to the Soblet - Sublett Family of Manakin Town, Virginia"; by Cameron Allen; *The American Genealogist*; Volume 75, No.2 [April 2000]

SOBLET see also **SUBLETT**

SUBLETT *The Sublettes: A Study of a Refugee Family in the 18th Century*; by D. B. Nunis, Jr; np; nd.

SOBLETT / SUBLET *The Soblett (Sublet) Family of Manakintown King William Parish, Virginia*; by Cameron Allen; Edited by James N. Jackson; Detroit; 1994

SUBLETT *Partial History of the French Huguenots by the Name Sublett at Manakin in Powhatan Co, VA*; by Samuel S. Sublett; np; 32pp; 1896

SUBLETT *Generations Remembered Sublette Family 1700-1850*; by Nancy Louise Sublett; np; nd.

SUBLET *The Kelly Family*; by Mrs John D. Moore, np; nd

SUBLETT *Partial History of the French Huguenots by name Sublets at Manakin in Powhatan County, VA* by Samuel S. Sublet; 32p; 1896

SUMATE *De La CHAUMETTE (Shumate)*; by Robert S. Riley; 1979; c.100p

SOUPLIE / SUPPLEE *The Sharple - Sharpless Family, Volume I and II*; by Bart Anderson, Editor; West Chester, PA; 1966

STELLE "Four Generations in America of the Huguenot Family of Stelle"; by Maud Burr Morris; *NYG&B Record* Vol XLIV,; (Apr 1913)

STRANGE *A Chart Showing Descendants of John Strange of Portsmouth, RI for four (4) Generations*; 8 x 20 nd

STRANGE *Biographical and Historical Sketches of the Stranges of America and Across the Seas*; By A.T. Strange; 145pp; 1911

STARBO see also TRABUE

STREING / STRANG / STRANGE *The Strang Genealogy*; by Josephine Frost; Brooklyn, NY, 1915

STREING / STRANG / STRANGE The Strangs of Westchester"; by Charles Alfred Strange; *NYG&B Record*; Vol XCVIII, No. 4; (Oct 1967)

ST JULIAN *The Julian Family*; by Frances Julian Hine; Winston Salem, NC; Sep 1974

ST JULIAN *The Rouths of Randolph County, NC*; by Lawrence W. Routh; np; nd.

ST JULIAN *The Julians and Allied Families*; by Elizabeth Cate Manley; Cleveland, TN; 1972

ST JULIAN *The Julian Family in Bohemia Manor Cecil County, Maryland*; by Rebecca Downey White; Jul 1945

de ST JULIAN "A Genealogy of the de St Julian Family of South Caroline"; by Paul R. Julian; *Transactions HSSC; No.105 [2001]*

STELLE *Pintard, Stelle Chronoloby includes VanVorst, Marselis, Hutchins*; by Tempe Fenn Crosby; 2000; Baton Rouge, LA

SY / SEE "New Information on the See and De Vaux Families"; by Glenna See Hill; *NYG&B Record* (Apr 1979)

T

TILLOU / TILSON *A Genealogy of a Cooley Family of Hunterdon County New Jersey and a Tillou Family of French Huguenots*; by Carola Bogardus; np; 1937.

66

TILLOU *The Tillou Family, East Orange Essex Co, NJ;* by Juliette Tillou; np ; nd

TRABUE *Colonial Men and Times: Containing: The Journal of Col Daniel Trabue, Some Accounts of His Ancestry, Life, and Travels in Virginia and the Present State of Kentucky, During the Revolutionary Period, The Huguenots, Genealogy, with Brief Sketches of Allied Families;* Ed. Lillie DuPuy Van Culin Harper; Philadelphia;1916

TRABUE / STARBO *Trabue Family in America 1700-1983;* by Julie Trabue Yates & Charles C. Trabue; Baltimore; 515pp; 1983

TRABUE *The Ancestry of Anthony Trabue (Antoine Trabuc);* by James D. Trabue; 1992; manuscript

TREGO *History of the Trego Family* by A. Trego Schertzer; np; nd

TREGO *Historical Account of the Trego Family;* by A. Shertzer; 1884; 144p

TREZENVANT *Trezenvant Family in the U. S. From the Arrival of Daniel, Huguenot at Charles Town, SC in 1685 to the Present;* by J. T. Trezevat; np; 1914

de TURK / DETURK *History and Genealogy of the DeTurk DeTurck Family, Descendants of Isaac De Turk and Maria De Harcourt;* by Eugene P. DeTurk; DeTurk Family Assn; 1934

V

VALLEAU *Valleau Genealogy;* by Mary E. Earle and Elinor E. Earle; np; nd.

VASSALL "The Vassalls of London and Jamaica"; by George E. McCracken; *Studies in Genealogy and Family History in Tribuate to Charles Evans On the Occasion of His Eightieth Birthday;* Edited by Lindsay L. Brook; Association for the Promotion of Scholarship in Genealogy, Ltd; Occasional Publication No, Two; 1989

VASSALS *Vassals of New England and Their Descendants*; by E. D. Harris; np; 26pp; 1862

VAUTRIN / WOTRING *The Wotring - Woodring Famly of Pennsylvania*; by Raymond Martin Bell & Mabel Ghering Grandquist; Washington, PA; 1968

de VEAUX *Genealogy of the DeVeaux Family*; by Thos F. DeVoe; np; 1885

VIA *Micajah Via Sr. of Albemarle County, Virginia and His Descendants 1740 - 1900*; by Judy Maupin Pons; Salem, OR; 1999

VIGNE *The Maiden Family of Virginia and Allied Families 1623-1991*; by Sarah Finch Maiden Rollins; Houston, Tx; 1991

VILLEPONTEUX "The Villeponteux Family of South Carolina"; by I. Howard Peck; *The South Carolina Historical Genealogical Magazine*; Vol 50; ____

VIVIAN "Vivian Family of Virginia"; by Charles Banks Heineman; Volume 5; *Genealogies of Virginia Families from the Virginia Magazine of History and Biography*; Baltimore; 1981

de VOS / de VEAUX *A Genealogy History of the Kolb, Kulp or Culp Family*; by Daniel Kolb Cassel; np; 1895

X

XAVIER / SEVIER *Sevier Family History and 28 Collateral Family Lineages*; by Cora Bales Sevier & Nancy S. Madden

Z

ZELLER *History of Zeller and Urich Families*; no author; Reading, PA nd [1920]

ZELLER / SELLAIRE "Zeller Family Revision"; by John F. Vallentine; *The Pennsylvania Genealogical Magazine*; Vol 27 No. 2 (1971)

A Book of Garretts, 1600 to 1960, Including Notes on the Following: Agee, Bogard, Bondarant, Burton, Cayce, Faure, Featherstone, Fuqua, Garrett, Glick, Jones, Maxey, Milby, Radford, Dallee, Vance, Victor, Waggoner, Whitlock, and Other Southern Families; by Hester Elizabeth Garrett; Lansing, MI; 1963

Turff & Twigg Volume One The French Land; by Priscilla Harris Cabel; Richmond, VA 1988

Huguenot Pedigrees; by Charles E. Lart; Volumes I and II; London; 1924/25; reprinted in one volume; Baltimore, MD; 1997

Appendix

Over the years many genealogies and family histories have been published that claimed a French or Huguenot connection, many with little or no documented proof. The majority of the claims were based on family tradition and the fact that the surname sounded French. Many a sad family historian who has discovered that there was little French or Huguenot blood in your vains. These lines continue to appear as claimed Huguenot lines and continue to be disaproved by the National Huguenot Society.

The following is a list of Genealogies that have at one time or another made a Huguenot claim and have been disqualified. The reason usually is that there is no proof that the claimed Ancestor had any documented connection with the French or Huguenot family. These lines are CLOSED and cannot be used or claimed as Huguenot.

BALLOU *An Elaborate History and Genealogy of the Ballous in America*; by Adin Ballou; 1888; 1324p.

BALLOU *Ballou In America, An Addendum to the Original History and Genealogy*; By Historical Records Survey, WPA; 1937; 210p.

BASYE *The Basye Family in the United States* by Otto Basye

BLANCHARD *The Mccurdy's of Nova Scotia - Genealogical Record & Biographical Sketches of....*; by H. Perry Blanchard; 1930

BLANCHARD *Family Gatherings Relating to the Smith and Blanchard Families. with a Memoir of the Rev Elias Smith Pastor of Middleton, Mass*; by George Peabody; Danvers, MA; 1929

BLANCHARD *Blanchards of Rhode Island*; by Adelaide Blanchard Crandall; np; nd

BLANCHARD *A Genealogical History of the Clark and Worth Families and other Puritan Settlers in the Massachusetts Bay Colony;* by Carol Clark Johnson, Privatly printed, 1970

70

BLANCHARD *A Blanchard Memorial being a brief account of our Ancestors as far as the writer has been able to trace them through the various Branches back to Colonial Times together with a short History of our own Family*; by Arthur William Blanchard; North Adams, MA; 1935

BLANCHARD *Commemorative of Calvin and Luther Blanchard Action Minute-men 1775*; by Alfred Sereno Hudson; West Acton, MA; 1899

BOUTON *Bouton - Boughton Family Descendants of John Bouton a Native of France*; by James Boughton; 1890

DANA *Memoranda of Some of the Descendants of Richard Dana of Cambridge*; by Rev John Jay Dana; 64p, 1865

DANA *The Dana Family in America*; by E. E. Dana; 685p; 1956

DANA *The Dana Saga: Three Centuries of the Dana Family in Cambridge*; by Henry W. L. Dana; 61p; 1941

DURFEE *The Descendants of Thomas Durfee of Portsmouth, RI*; by Wm F. Reed; Volume I Washington DC; 1902; Volume II Washington DC; 1905

DEVANE *De Vanes 1798 - 1975*; by Kissam P. De Vane & others ; Moultrie, GA; nd

DEVANE *William R. King and His KIn*; by Henry Poellnitz JOhnson, Sr; Birmingham, AL; 1975

FILLOW/ FILLO *A Record of the Descendants of John Fillow A Huguenot Refugee from France*; by D. H. Van Hoosak; Albany, NY; 1888

LAMAR / LAMORE "Thomas Lamar of the Province of Maryland and a Part of his Descendants"; by William Harmony Lamar; *Publication of the Southern History Association*; Vol I Washington, DC; 1897

MERRILL *A Merrill Memorial An Account of the Descendants of Nathaniel Merrill and Early Settler of Newbury, Mass*; by Samuel Merrill; Cambridge, MA; 1917-1928

OSTRANDER *A Genealogy History of the Stephen Ostrander of the Ostrander Family in America, 1660-1902*; by Ogden H. Ostrander; 1902 (One folio sheet folded)

PATTEE "Peter Pattee of Haverhill, Massachusetts: A "Journey Shoemaker" and his Descendants"; By Marie Lollo Scalise and Virginia M. Ryan; *NEG&H Register*; Volume CXLVI; Oct 1992

ROYER *History of Christopher Royer & His Posterity* (in Gift, Kern, Royer Genealogy); by A.K. Gift; n.p., 1909

ROYER *Genealogical Records of the Royer Family in America*; by Rev J. G. Francis; Lebanon, PA; 1928

ROYER *The Royer Family*; by W. Roy Metz & Floyd G. Hoestine; PA; 1951

SABIN *The Descendants of William Sabin of Rehoboth Massachusetts*; Compiled by Gordon Alan Moore & Thomas J. & Dixie Prittie; nd [1995?]

SABIN *The Sabin Family of America The Four Earliest Generations*; by Rev Anson Titus, Jr; Weymouth, MA; 1882

SABIN *Ancestors, Descendants and Relatives of Carlton Sabin and his wives, including Contemporary Cousins and In Laws*; by Sabin Crocker, Sr; 1971

SANTEE *Genealogy of the Santee Family in America*; by Ellis M. Santee; Cortland, NY; 1899; 211pp, 1927

SANTEE *Santee Genealogy Volume Numbers 1-4 & Volume Numbers 1 & 2*; by Ellis M. Santee; 4pages each 1899-1901

STRODE / STROUD *Strode - Strode Families in England and America*; by James S. Elston; np; 123pp; 1949

STRODE / STROUD *Strode - Strode Families in England and America*; by James S. Elston; Volume II; np; 165pp; 1970

STRODE / STROUD *Strode - Strode Families in England and America*; by James S. Elston; Volume III; np; 144pp; 1973

STRODE / STROUD *Strode - Strode Families in England and America*; by James S. Elston; Volume IV; 31pp; 1976

STRODE *In Search of the Strode Orphans Ancestry of Edward Strode, Jeremiah Strode, Samuel Strode and Martha (Strode) Bryan*; by David C. McMurtry, Michael L. Kallam, Kerry Ross O'Boran; Lexington, KY; 1998

VINCENT *The Downers of America with Genealogical Record*; by David R. Downer Neward, NJ; 1900

VINTON *The Vinton Memorial Comprising A Genealogy of the Descendants of John Vinton of Lynn 1648: Also Genealogical sketches of several Allied Families*; by John A. Vinton; Boston; 1858